Routledge Revivals

Development Technology

The problem of economic development in the Global South was recognized as one of the defining challenges of the twentieth century. Professor Duller, a Dutch economist who worked in advisory and research capacities across various developing nations, demonstrates in *Development Technology* (originally published in 1982) how these challenges could be addressed through the application of specially designed or adapted technology.

The author observes that development planners had been misled by apparent parallels between nineteenth-century Western industrialization and late twentieth-century conditions in third world countries. While Western industrialization drew its workforce from agriculture during periods of low demographic growth and high industrial employment, the Global South faced different circumstances: rapidly increasing populations and modern technologies that provided limited employment opportunities. The strategies advocated since the 1950s had largely failed to achieve self-sustained economic growth in these nations.

Professor Duller argues that the solution remained technological but required a radically new approach that responded to the actual conditions prevailing in much of the developing world.

Development Technology

H.J. Duller

Routledge
Taylor & Francis Group

First published in 1982
by Routledge & Kegan Paul Ltd

This edition first published in 2026 by Routledge
4 Park Square, Milton Park, Abingdon, Oxon, OX14 4RN

and by Routledge
605 Third Avenue, New York, NY 10158

Routledge is an imprint of the Taylor & Francis Group, an informa business

Publisher's Note
The publisher has gone to great lengths to ensure the quality of this reprint but points out that some imperfections in the original copies may be apparent.

Disclaimer
The publisher has made every effort to trace copyright holders and welcomes correspondence from those they have been unable to contact.

For Product Safety Concerns and Information please contact our EU representative GPSR@taylorandfrancis.com. Taylor & Francis Verlag GmbH, Kaufingerstraße 24, 80331 München, Germany

A Library of Congress record exists under LCCN: 82003688

ISBN: 978-1-041-26811-6 (hbk)
ISBN: 978-1-003-75171-7 (ebk)
ISBN: 978-1-041-26854-3 (pbk)

Book DOI 10.4324/9781003751717

Development technology

H. J. Duller
Professor of Social Science
University of Leiden

Routledge & Kegan Paul
London, Boston, Melbourne and Henley

First published in 1982
by Routledge & Kegan Paul Ltd
39 Store Street, London WC1E 7DD,
9 Park Street, Boston, Mass. 02108, USA,
296 Beaconsfield Parade, Middle Park,
Melbourne, 3206, Australia and
Broadway House, Newtown Road,
Henley-on-Thames, Oxon RG9 1EN
Printed in Great Britain by
Redwood Burn Ltd, Trowbridge, Wiltshire

Library of Congress Cataloging in Publication Data

Duller, H. J.

Development technology.
(International library of anthropology)
Bibliography: p.
Includes index.
1. Technical assistance. 2. Economic development.
3. Underdeveloped areas—Unemployment. I. Title.
II. Series.
HC60.D796 338.9'009172'4 82–3688

ISBN 0–7100–0990–9 AACR2

Contents

1	Between technology and intermediate technology	1
2	Fashionable modernity	7
3	The origin of originality	13
4	The crises and the cycles	19
5	The temptations of economies of scale	25
6	Impediments to omniscience	54
7	Basic needs for the needy	64
8	Income distribution and redistribution	70
9	Alternatives	78
10	Contradictions and dependences	83
11	Unemployment and idleness	92
12	Productivity	103
13	Tarnished inheritance	111
14	Corruptible progress	128
15	Development propensity	143
16	Development expertise	150
17	Development possibility	163
	Bibliography	173
	Index	191

1 Between technology and intermediate technology*

> 'Societies can be looked upon as primitive or advanced according to the level of their technological achievement.' (Dickson)

In countries where the sun shines more often than here in Europe - the poor, underdeveloped, often tropical and usually former colonial areas - there is, under that sun, nothing new as far as the adaptation of technology is concerned, at least not as much as the Western advocates of this latest approach to the problem of poverty profess. In all countries people use resources and aids to extract more from nature than it would otherwise yield. The aids are aimed at and adapted to the fulfilment of existing needs. They are the result of - and adapted to - existing technical design capacity. Locally available materials are used and processed for consumption or further production. Following the pattern of wealth created elsewhere by industrial means, the desire to consume more is aroused; and so more needs to be produced. But the traditional technologies are less suited to meet rising expectations of wealth.

THE SCENARIO OF CONVERGENCE

The first time I encountered an adapted technology - although it was not yet called by that name - was in the spring of 1968, at midnight, in a *bidonville* outside Dakar. The Senegalese development planner driving the car lost his way in the labyrinth of alleys between the ramshackle huts. There was no room to reverse. Then

* I would like to acknowledge help with the translation from Harry Drost MA in association with First Edition, Cambridge.

there appeared in the glow of the headlights a long row of iron bedsteads, evidently the production line of a bed-welding works. Gas and oxygen cylinders were placed informally against an as yet unfinished bedhead. And behind it lay a heap of scrap and gas piping, recycled more than once, judging by the degree of oxidization: the stocks of raw materials.

'Here they make the beds', said the lost planner, still without appreciation (which by now he probably has) of this ecological, organic, intermediate, alternative and decentralizing element of the process of production, the tangible outcome of which was holding us up. In 1968 these small-scale activities were seen primarily as obstacles to progress. Progress meant industrialization, preferably 'heavy', and investment planning, preferably 'rational'. Tinkering with scrap iron was thought to be at best marginal, a transitional phenomenon between the chisel of the primitive craftsman and the computer terminal with which post-industrial man regulates the cybernetic production processes.

A society reaches the *post*-industrial stage when extensive rationalization and automation has effected such a dramatic increase in labour productivity that a thinly manned production apparatus can produce the whole range of useful and necessary, or even unnecessary, consumer goods. The labour force, released from the burden of hard physical labour in an earlier phase of mechanization, is gradually released from the industrial treadmill and transferred to the service sector. A pleasant life in the sphere of art, culture, and social welfare, 'a choice of ways of life and modes of living, a choice of leisure-time distraction which the most privileged of our forefathers would have found most bewildering' is in the offing (International Labour Office, 1972, 26). This kind of saturation was in the 1960s euphorically proclaimed as a goal both desirable and within the reach of a development strategy. Rostow illustrated the historical line of development with an analogy from horse-racing. One had to imagine a race with some white and some black horses. The black horses were handicapped and were lagging behind. But because they were racing on the same course as the white horses they were advancing towards the same finishing line.

The lesson to be learnt was clear: he might take a bit longer, but eventually our black fellow would arrive at the finish. Then he too would have the latest car at the front of his house and a swimming pool at the back. Kahn, who at the time of euphoria was compiling quantitatively based scenarios plotting the advent of the Golden

Age, was optimistic as late as 1976: 'We expect that almost all countries will develop the characteristics of super- and post-industrial societies' (Kahn et al., 1976, 1).

The notion of a common final stage towards which (economic) history is moving is also taken up in so-called convergence theory, which assumes a coalescence of capitalist and socialist economic systems. The capitalist economy, it is argued, is subject to ever more government control; the socialist governments, in contrast, have come to recognize the benefits of the market mechanism. And since in this vision there is no healthier economy than a mixed economy, the outcome of historical development in these two apparently divergent systems is the healthiest economy conceivable - ensuring the greatest prosperity for the population. Artists, who are allegedly peculiarly sensitive to future developments, made it their task to give concrete form to the city of the future, in which - since hardly anyone would need to work - recreational facilities were given pride of place. Models of the New Babylon designed by the Dutch painter Constant were put on display in progressive art galleries; a new Golden Age was solemnly proclaimed.

Technological progress was seen as the driving force behind this gratifying advance.

> Mankind has risen from a man-powered technology to a low-energy technology (based on wood-fire, wind, water, plant and animal power) to a high-energy technology based on fossil fuels, to a potentially unlimited-energy technology based on the promise that the fission power of breeder reactors will enable us to contrive fusion power that in turn will give us enough energy to use any material whatsoever (Watson, 1975, 487).

As long as there was no doubt at home that the above promise would be redeemed, the dispensing of the same technology abroad was considered a matter of course. The then prevalent logic of technologically oriented development aid was simple. The developing countries are poor because they possess neither the equipment nor the technical skills to employ it. They will require both if they are to provide greater prosperity for their populations. This is their proclaimed goal. So we, who have gone through the development process and possess the requisite skills and equipment, will have to pass them on to these countries to speed the desired development on its way.

The bubble burst initially abroad, but soon afterwards it burst at home as well. For a start, while the literature of development economics prescribed capital-intensive production processes for the areas outside the wide sphere of America and Europe, the actual investments were, for a variety of reasons that will be discussed in the following chapters, not always made with great circumspection.

The automatic hen battery whose jamming conveyor belts broke the eggs, a case reported by Van Nieuwenhuijze from Egypt, is a striking example of a misadventure rarely reported in the literature of development economics, but mentioned, all the more often for that, in dinner-table anecdotes (1976, 527).

'Give us the jobs and we'll finish the tools' - such Churchillian irony is indicative of what would later be called 'maladjustment'. The warnings of the development economists should have been heeded from the start. They had already recognized that an advanced industrial technology is not suitable for countries where wages are low and labour abundant.

HOLLAND SHOWS THE WAY

Thereupon the model builders arose. While Kahn talked contentedly of accelerated development, depicted in graphs and curves which only seemed to end because they had reached the top of the page, Forrester and Meadows inveighed against exponential growth. Everything on earth is finite, in their mind, and therefore all things must come to an end, including all good things, such as the ever-improving standard of living. In Holland, where many had only recently suppressed the concept of unrestricted consumption as sinful, the idea of the limits to growth immediately struck root. Holland would show the world that it took zero-growth seriously. Politicians, at heart enamoured of the ethic of abstinence, could once more openly affirm the virtue of thrift.

If OPEC, intent on increasing its profits, had at that point not raised drastically the price of oil and in addition announced an oil embargo of Holland (a reprisal for that country's alleged pro-Israeli stance), then the fashionable view would probably have survived no longer than many another fad - a couple of months' front-page news, then a slow percolation through to higher, middle and lower (educational) levels of society. As it was, the fear of finiteness has stuck. Nevertheless, energy consumption in Holland has risen steadily ever since (despite a number of new oil-price rises); and when the economy actually showed signs of flagging, the politicians of zero-growth have taken recourse to the traditional Keynesian remedies. Yet the aversion to industrial technology has remained, although a different mainspring is responsible for this. 'Men make tools, but in another and equally important sense, it is also true that tools make men' (Feibleman, 1967, 332). The notion that technology not only determines the standard of living but equally our way of life, and that, in this respect, modern industrial technology has taken a wrong turning, is a recurring contemporary theme which will be discussed in subsequent chapters. Against this background the compromise idea of an intermediate technology becomes respectable. It combines the two beliefs that technical means are necessary to sustain life, and that at a certain, though indeterminate, point of development, our way of life is unfavourably affected by them. Intermediate technology, then, is to contain the advantages of the developed while avoiding the pitfalls of the overdeveloped.

In point of fact, the rich countries have shown little inclination to experiment in their own backyard with these humane, liberating, peaceful technologies, with technologies for the people, the village, or the 'small scale' in general. Their application here is, after all, likely to stunt economic growth, whose material rewards are held in high esteem by politicians and constituents alike. Restraint may admittedly be morally salutary in the long run but, as Keynes observed, in the long run we are all dead. That the interests of the people of the Third World are better served by self-restraint is a rather more acceptable proposition as far as the prosperous West is concerned.

The creation of wealth relies on technological innovation. In order that the poor countries could tap this source of progress, they were enjoined to adopt the technology of the highly developed industrial - and now post-industrial - world.

But apart from the fact that the model of Western economic development which has long been held up as a shining example was finally discredited by the oil crisis and other setbacks, the concept of 'progress' was also reexamined in the West itself. Technology and industry were taken to task for their harmful effects on employment and the environment. There was even some talk of 'deindustrialization' (Blackaby, 1979). But because the majority, habituated to prosperity, refused to embrace the notion of abstinence, a compromise was found in zero-growth - a situation of constancy that anyway seemed naturally suited to the Third World. The theme of adapted technology was incorporated into the orchestration of development economics. The first Institutes were founded and the first chairs in development economics were established.

2 Fashionable modernity

> 'Just as fashion setters emphasize, display and conceal at different times different parts of the female anatomy (though presumably all are there all the time) so economic and social research tends to be preoccupied with different aspects of the social system' (Kahn)

The road to prosperity and wealth is known - it has been travelled by the countries now rich as a result of industrialization. The terms 'underdeveloped', 'less developed' and 'developing' used for the poor countries already imply a strategy of imitation: the Third World can orient itself on the growth path taken by the Western economies. Depending on the progress made, the developing country is defined as being in a starting position, in a situation of self-accelerating growth, or in a phase of mass consumption, which the post-industrial West has meanwhile achieved. This road, however bumpy, can be travelled in less time than it took the industrialized countries, for the errors of navigation committed then are known and thus can be avoided. In addition, the superior technology is immediately available, to be applied in the most advanced form.

Therefore the developing countries are at an advantage. This assertion is corroborated by statistical evidence: the economies of the poor countries are growing more rapidly than did the economies of the now rich in their hesitant initial phase of development.

CONSUMPTION VERSUS CONTEMPLATION

The countries where technical-industrial development has advanced so far that a vanguard of social science experts has denoted them 'post-industrial' comprise the Rich West. At one time these countries, by today's standards, were poor. But whatever faults can be found with their social and economic systems, it is undeniable that the majority of the populations of these countries is rather better off than any other in the world. This may well be an anomaly whose days are numbered. The finiteness of natural resources and raw materials, the imminent collapse of the economic system, the transgression of even the social limits to growth - all these mark Western prosperity as a condition of *over*development, whose end is probable or even desirable. These complaints are rarely heard outside the Western world with the exception of Japan - which proves that, there, development efforts have borne fruit!

In the economically underdeveloped countries one can hear an occasional call for introspection and reflection on the relativity of material gratification. Some of the leaders speaking thus hope to do their country a service by curtailing middle-class consumption in favour of reinforcing its military potential; others are inspired by a philosophy of life which rejects unrestrained consumption and embraces contemplation. In Burma, Schumacher became so spell-bound by Buddhism that, as legend has it, he worked an eight-hour day for this religion after having put in an eight-hour day for the United Nations. In fact, Schumacher has given disproportionate support to the case of those in the rich countries who strive for the reduction of material wealth.

Gandhi's views on this matter are known. Yet he also spoke of the desirability of economic advance. 'If we tap all our resources, I am quite sure we can again be the richest country in the world' (Alvares, 1975, 135). I will not linger on the image evoked by the first part of this sentence, which seems strikingly discordant with the present-day conservationist alternative of the good life. More poignant is the second part, which expresses the vision of India as the richest nation in history, although the term 'rich' should not be interpreted in Schumacher's UN's statistical terms. One may wonder to what extent formerly colonial countries were indeed prosperous in the past; and if they were not, at least not in any vulgar economic sense, then why they did not draw on their resources to provide their people with a stronger material base on which, as has also been argued, a culture in the non-material sense could be grafted. There are two possible answers to this: either not every culture will admit of such development, or colonialism checked it. It is plausible that notions of being and of wellbeing in certain cultures cannot be easily reconciled with the yearly increase of the flow of products, which until recently was generally considered the highest good in the rich countries. Whether the obsession with growth has contaminated the purity of non-Western philosophy or whether the cultural trait of maximization, which economists at times seem to treat as a universal, here prevails - the fact remains that the representatives of the former colonies blame their poverty on the rich.

Poverty in this conception is caused by straightforward plunder. It is alleged that Western investments during the Industrial Revolution were financed with the profits made in the exploitation of the colonies. Admittedly not all poor countries are former colonies, nor are all formerly colonizing countries now rich, but it does not seem too farfetched to argue that the colonial period did not bring the white man merely burdens. Moreover, even when industrial investments in the colonies were not made solely for the benefit of the mother country, the resultant factory products deprived - perhaps unintentionally - the local craftsmen of their business, thereby stifling what indigenous economic activity existed. And in the post-industrial era, too, development aid for Western-inspired industrialization can act - perhaps unintentionally - as a disincentive for countries to follow their own, more appropriate, development goals, which may well deviate from the Western ideal. Such are the views emphatically put forward by the radicals. Attitudes towards international aid, which has been sold to taxpayers as both a political and a humanitarian gesture, have changed. Where development economists ten years ago still engaged in such hyperbole as '... never in history have voluntary transfers of capital of this magnitude ...', a moderate author recently imputed at least a 'déjà-vu look' to the donors (Schiavo-Campo and Singer, 1970, 245). This is convenient partly because the aforementioned taxpayers seem to have become susceptible to 'aid fatigue', which is sometimes explained by the absence of the spectacular results that apparently had been expected. The opinion has gained ground that, in spite of all development aid, the developing countries have fallen further behind, and even worse, aid itself is partly to blame. 'We have come to the paradoxical conclusion', writes Van Bronckhorst, 'that the efforts of development aid have had at least one measurable result: the progressive deterioration of the situation in large areas of the world' (Van Bronckhorst, 1976, 6).

THE LEAP FORWARD

Comparative material has been published recently by Lipton (1977, 28ff.). He observes that the poor countries have enjoyed a period of unprecedented growth; income per head has doubled in real terms over the last twenty-five years. Accepting UN definitions, he uses as the criterion of economic underdevelopment an income per head per year of $ 500 at 1960 prices and $ 750 at 1974 prices. Developing countries increased output by 2.6 per cent per year in the 1950s, and by 3 per cent per year in the 1960s. Lipton estimates the real rise in output per head from 1950 to 1970 at 75 per cent. What is more, 'the poor countries of the world have increased their productive capacity per head, through both physical capital equipment and "human capital" in the form of skills, faster than the income-per-head growth rates.' This does not mean that Lipton is now satisfied; his criticisms are levied at the skewed distribution of the increased wealth, which will be discussed later.

Another development economist of the earliest days, Singer, shares Lipton's view:

> The growth of aggregate production in the underdeveloped countries on average has been quite high in the last two decades and compares well with rates achieved even by countries like Japan, Canada and Australia at critical stages in their development history (Singer, 1972, 119).

The last comparison is redolent of the notion that there are advantages to being a latecomer. Those who start later, the argument runs, know what path to follow and can use the best means available. In general terms it is indeed easier to attempt to attain a goal which can be seen to be attainable. One will have learned from others' mistakes, and they can be anticipated and avoided. Moreover, the methods employed will certainly have been improved upon; the earlier, more haphazard, versions can be missed out. In this way of thinking it is to be expected that the countries industrializing later will develop faster than their historical examples. Such an accelerated development is closely linked to the technology chosen for modern industrialization. The contribution of technological advance to economic development will be examined in a subsequent chapter. Suffice it to say for the moment that it is evidently a powerful motor in the development process. Now that the latest and most advanced technical means in the industrial arsenal are available, it should not be surprising that development is accelerated. But it is already some time ago that this line of thought was dominant; the analysis has been altered considerably since, and the most recent critics have expounded very much the opposite view. For latecomers have to choose technologies that correspond to their precarious starting position, and they still have to follow the whole road followed by those that have had an earlier start. This historicist vision was implicit in many conceptions of development prevalent in the 1950s and 1960s, and is set down in the famous Pearson report.

HISTORICAL ANALYSIS

Rostow's postulation of the five stages which a country has to pass through before it reaches the level of the advanced industrial nations constitutes the epitome of this particular form of prescription for development. From the early phase, the 'traditional society', via 'take-off' and 'drive to maturity', a country becomes not only mature but above all more modern. The economy comes to resemble that of the 'free West' until it is indistinguishable from it; it has reached the last stage, 'the age of high mass consumption'. This process of elevation is called 'modernization'. Similar changes occur in all countries, for even the modern ones have not yet reached the goal; they are still becoming more and more modern. And again technology is seen as the great lever.

'Modernization is the transformation of the world by technology' (Berger, Berger and Kellner, 1974, 15). Aid to the underdeveloped should therefore consist mainly of transfer of technology. To this purpose President Truman promulgated a 'bold new program' of technical assistance, to ensure that all would enter what President Johnson would subsequently call the 'Great Society'. For the advanced countries this meant that the extent of progress could be inferred from the sums spent on research and development - or R & D, as it is often simply called - of new and newer technology.

The message for the beginners was that their technical capacity had to be expanded. That there were considerable discrepancies in the relative scarcities of labour and capital between the various stages of development was a point raised by only a few economists - 'ritual noises', Cooper called them (1972, 1).

In the historical phase of colonial domination the creation of wealth of the so-called mother country was the ultimate goal. The economies of the overseas territories were made subservient to this goal, and their economies were only allowed to develop if the interests of the mother country were not adversely affected. In the post-colonial era, too, international development aid has been organized on terms that protected the economic interests of the donors, and the stimulation of the recipient economies has not necessarily been of prime concern. The transfer of modern technology significantly spurs industrial activity in the donor country; it also tallies with the precept of theoretical economics that accelerated industrialization is the best strategy for prosperous economic development.

3 The origin of originality

'Political economy is a dismal science.' (Carlyle)

In his historical development man has devised gradually more complicated tools. Technology is sometimes seen to be so essential to the human mode of existence that the line between man and animal is drawn at the conscious use of technical aids. When an ape, witnessed by excited biologists, fits the parts of a fishing rod together in order to reach a banana put outside his cage, he is admired for his ingenuity. His initiative could indeed be construed as a modification of the traditional line of demarcation; he comes one step nearer to man. In any case he avails himself of a means to satisfy a need which otherwise he would have to forgo. This is the essential aspect of technology: privation is pushed back, the effort required to sustain life is reduced. That is why technology is often described as the blessing that adds dignity to human life.

THE SPIRIT OF CARLYLE DISPELLED

It is striking how social thought forever returns to technology as the source, sometimes of all good, sometimes of all evil, and sometimes, in a sense, of everything.... Forbes sees man as liberating himself in history from his animal existence by harnessing the forces of nature. 'Technology begins with man, the first toolmaking primate' (1968, 3). An animal may at times use a random stone to crack a shell but half a million years ago Peking man began to look for particular stones for particular purposes and to give them a particular form. As seen from this angle, the use of tools is certainly essential to man and society. Admittedly, technology does not free man from nature-imposed limitations, but the acquisition of means that make life comfortable, even possible, is much facilitated. Here Forbes employs a phrase which also inspires the advertisements for new domestic appliances: 'liberation from drudgery'. The heavy work is taken out of our hands; there is less need to work our fingers to the bone to earn a living. For Locke, nature offered an inexhaustible abundance for inquisitive man to act upon, for him to subject ever more to his needs.

But the boon of technology also has a dark side, and this is discussed hardly less eagerly in the literature. Technology may be essential to man, but his human essence is in turn influenced by the technology he himself has developed. That in this way technology determines the organization of society is a widely held view, shared, for instance, by the non-marxist authors referred to in this discussion. Many writers have pursued this further and have uncovered the negative, the 'alienating' aspect of technology. This will be discussed in a subsequent chapter. For the moment it is interesting to note that this different line of thought also assumes a degree of parallel development in societies, in so far as they apply comparable technologies. If these technologies are of decisive importance, then their influence will eventually push these societies in the same direction, to the point where a world-embracing culture of McLuhan's 'global village' is imminent - although McLuhan's is a far cry from the new village culture envisaged in radical thought. Ayres, in the 1930s, had already described mechanisms of this kind in his theory of economic progress which assumed that the 'tool-using process' would expand exponentially and so initiate the spectacular development which the economies of the countries where this process took place have indeed experienced. The element of succession is further related to the peculiarity that an innovation often combines earlier technologies. After the wheel came not the internal-combustion engine but the cart. The naming of an innovation then shows traces of the combination effected, oddly enough sometimes as a negation, as in wireless telegraphy, or the horseless carriage.

It is understandable that often technological progress is accepted without reservation as a great blessing. After all, it allows the production of more of the desired goods with less effort, and new goods are deemed desirable if only because they are new. The Economic Principle, explained on the first pages of every textbook as the principle according to which the means to achieve a specific end should be minimized, or alternatively, a given end should maximize the means, seems to operate here on either side of the definition. This fills the authors of such books with great pleasure. 'The ghost of Carlyle', writes Samuelson, 'should be relieved to know that economics, after all, has not been a dismal science - in the advanced world' (1976, 733). Even Marcuse apparently appreciated that technological progress is a positive factor, because it seems to be the prerequisite for any humanitarian advance (Brouwer and Hiedema, 1975, 9). This touches upon another aspect of the phenomenon, namely the reduction of the working day made possible by technology. This creates greater scope for self-development - hitherto a prerogative of the rich and the leisured. All this, though far from unanimously accepted, has created a consensus - eclipsed only recently - that technology is essentially a positive phenomenon. This attitude shone through even in the debate on ecological balance, when several quarters suggested that contemporary problems could be solved by designing new technologies which eliminated the disadvantages but retained the advantages of the old technologies.

The predilection for the new, the advanced, and the labour-saving is generally considered to be peculiarly American. This can be explained by the fact that the American Dream has been realized within a few generations. For most Americans progress has been very visible: they live longer, healthier, better and safer lives, and all this has been achieved comparatively recently, for today's adults still remember the poverty of their grandparents. Technological advances have been, moreover, very tangible in the daily life of the majority of people in America, which in 1900 was a far more rural country than Britain. In their youth, today's American adults witnessed the revolution in agriculture as a result of the introduction of new harvesting machines. While at the end of the First World War 25 per cent of the American labour force was engaged in the agricultural sector, this figure had dwindled to 4 per cent in 1976 - and this small number of farmers produced more than enough foodstuffs to supply the entire country. It seems unthinkable that, as advocates of zero-growth sometimes contend, this expansion must come to an end. It is indeed exponential, as is shown in the reduction of the period allowed for depreciation of assets: improved technology reduces the variable costs of the new machine, and the point where the total costs of the new production method fall below just the variable costs of the old comes ever sooner. And less time lapses between the invention of a new technique and its application. Rosenberg provides a survey which shows that since the middle of the last century the incubation period, meaning the interval between invention and innovation, has been cut from 79 years (for the fluorescent lamp in 1859) to 56 years (for the gyro-compass in 1908) to 10 years (for the turbo-jet engine in 1934) to 5 years (for streptomycine in 1944).

EXPLORING THE PAST

In the last few decades there has been a revival in the study of the history of technology. In Britain, Singer published his five-volume 'History of Technology'; and departments specializing in the history of technology have been established at the University of Bath and the Imperial College in London. In the United States, the Society for the History of Technology was founded, and it began to publish the journal 'Technology and Culture'. In Germany, the Soviet Union and in Sweden the subject has also aroused scholarly interest.

In general outline, the history of technology is known. From having been initially based on the energy of human muscle-power, technology developed via wood-fire, wind and water power, and the energy of draught animals, to a technology based on fossil fuels. Forbes points out that this development was adapted in different areas of the world to fit particular natural and economic conditions. In China and India technology took a different course than in the West. It is known that a number of important inventions were first applied in the oriental countries. In ancient China cast iron was produced; drilling brine was common, and natural gas was piped to heat the salt pans; windmills powered irrigation pumps; stirrups were in use, and the collar harness made animal traction more efficient than in Europe; silk reeling and paper manufacture were practised; and the magnetic compass was used in navigation. These techniques were probably developed autonomously, cultural diffusion playing no role.

But in recent history the adoption of foreign technologies seems to have been the norm. In the phase of the ascendancy of fossil fuels as major sources of energy, the example of industrialization in Britain served as the model. In the light of present-day ecological objections one may wonder whether the adaptation made at that time has been an ideal choice! Bhatt observes that the level of development of the populations of Germany and the United States was higher rather than lower than that of Britain when they followed her industrial example. It is unlikely that the energy sources and the other factors of production would have been present in the same scarcity, and therefore price relationships, in all these countries

(1975, 563). 'Mis-adaptation' must have occurred. Incidentally, the British government tried to prevent the transfer of technology by prohibiting the export of machines, but to no avail. Locomotives in particular were reproduced at such a rate that a whole industry was quickly formed. During these transfers foreign experts were hired, or local technicians were sent out to study the inventions. In 1872 Carnegie visited the Bessemer steelworks in England to study the production methods used there. Upon his return to the United States he evidently applied them with success: the rise of the American steel industry dates from this period. American steel production increased so rapidly that in 1900 the output of American furnaces was almost double that of Britain and France. Then British and German technicians travelled to the United States to discover how labour productivity had been trebled there (Gruber, 1969, 41). Mutual contact between countries setting up specific industries and copying techniques originated elsewhere has been a crucial factor in the development of the Western economies. The latest latecomer in this respect is Sweden, which until the end of the last war was still largely dependent on forestry and mining. It has since generated great wealth with the erection of an industrial apparatus based on foreign technology, and presently occupies one of the top positions in the income-per-head table.

Recent studies have thrown up the question whether the continuity of growth on such an unprecedented scale may not be constrained by the availability of energy resources. This indeed is an important consideration. It is a criterion that has been used to classify societies: they are designated as traditional if they are dependent primarily on living energy sources, which alleviate human labour only marginally, the level of technology remaining more or less constant. Economists call this a constant production function; according to Rostow, this is characteristic of 'traditional' society.

The issue turns on the question of the relationship between what is required to manufacture a product and what can be derived from the resulting commodity. Only when there remains a surplus does the possibility arise of directing part of the energy sources away from the demands of immediate consumption towards initiating a further development, namely the production of capital goods. Historically, the engineering craft has been the driving force behind Western industry.

Stewart provides figures which illustrate the advancing level of capitalization. With capital stock per head in 1920 = 100, the figure for Britain would be 125 in 1930,

129 in 1950 and 210 in 1970. For the United States, with 1920 = 100, the value of capital stock per head was 61 in 1900, 206 in 1940 and 341 in 1950 (Stewart, 1974, 24). And since the intensity of deployment of capital goods is of overwhelming influence on labour productivity, the latter rose accordingly: if the average for the period 1890-99 is set at 100, labour productivity in Britain rose to 104 in 1900, and 171 in 1960; and for the United States the rise was more dramatic, from 110 in 1910 to 381 in 1960. The concomitant rise in wages is even more staggering: with again 1890-99 = 100, the figure for Britain would be 104 in 1900 and 219 in 1960; and for the United States 110 in 1900 and 381 in 1960 (Phelps-Brown, 1973). After all, increase in income is the objective of a strategy for economic development.

The concepts and calculations used above are typical of economics and economists. The next chapter, therefore, will examine how theoretical economics has dealt with technology in the course of its development, when the main concern was to explain the industrial growth of the West and no one was concerned with the consequences of the transfer of the trusted technology to economically less developed countries.

There can be no doubt that industrial technology has been a major contributor to the generation of historically unprecedented material wealth now experienced by those who have conceived this technology. But because society dominated by technology has non-material traits which are thought to be undesirable, there is no general rejoicing. Moreover, non-renewable natural resources are heavily overused; for this reason a repeat performance of the exhaustive Western industrialization process on a world-wide scale is impracticable. Countries which are not yet industrialized therefore had better not strive for the adoption of an unchanged Western technology.

4 The crises and the cycles

> 'For many economists technical change is still manna from heaven.' (Cooper)

It is clear to anyone who observes his own (modern) society that technology has determined its character to a very large extent. A Western country devoid of, or even with a reduced number of tools, vehicles and aeroplanes, is inconceivable and a Westerner would find life there impossible. Yet the social sciences in general and economics in particular have long neglected the phenomenon of technology. The mistake of all classical economists, who predicted either a stationary state or inevitable crises, may be attributed to this negligence. Malthus's prognosis that over time the means of subsistence would lag behind the natural growth of population, for instance, proved false because he underestimated technical inventiveness.

Even after technology had been incorporated into the economic paradigm, interest continued to be focused on the cyclical movements caused by the fluctuating levels of investment in industry and employment. Economists were still more interested in the business cycle than in the developmental trend, which, however much interrupted by fluctuations, asserted itself more and more.

THE HOMEOPATHIC ECONOMY

Why is it that in the past economic theory has shown so little interest in technology? Even though it was recognized that the resolution of problems of scarcity - which is after all what economics is all about - clearly involved the use of resources and aids, and above all their efficient use through technology, this influence was nevertheless consigned to the theoretical periphery. It was a prior condition that need not be investigated further: a datum. A datum is assumed to remain constant, and if, as in the case of technology, this should not be so, then the factor is raised to the level of variable, but not quite a variable within the field of explanation. In this mode of analysis it is impossible for technology to be treated as a manipulative factor which leads the striving for wealth in a certain direction.

In recent years this has certainly changed. Those economists who advocate a 'limit' to technology have recognized that technological development is of overriding importance, though they consider it undesirable. And those economists who support the introduction of a specific technology to effect all kinds of eagerly awaited social changes equally seem to attribute great power to the unexplained variable.

Incidentally, the initial reluctance of economic theory can also be explained by this social science's aversion to dealing with social phenomena, which, unlike natural phenomena - the natural scientific mode of explanation has always been the model of economic theory - do not lend themselves very easily to objectifying quantification.

The 'creative response', as Schumpeter called it, which society finds to the specific problems of resource allocation and scarcity is neither explained nor predicted by economics. To this extent an economist urging a developing country to accept a kind of intermediate technology acts as a homeopathist writing out a prescription - small quantities of the active ingredient may alleviate the condition.

When development economists make pronouncements like 'Underlying the receptivity of a country to the diffusion of a new technology is the rationality of the culture' and 'Basic to the speed of learning is the desire to learn', one is tempted to dismiss their 'cure' as a layman's panacea (Kindleberger, 1965, 148).

EXPULSION AND COMPENSATION

Those who adhere to traditional economic theory adhere to Adam Smith or, if they are of a more radical bent, Karl Marx. Smith described with evident praise a pin factory where an advance had been made because (a) time was saved by the change-over from one to another operation, (b) the workers became more adept at learning their detailed tasks, and (c) machines were designed which 'facilitate and abridge labour'.

Marx here again proved to be the last of the classical economists. He borrowed Smith's analysis, but pointed out that there is a limit to the division of labour in that tasks cannot be split indefinitely, and in any case there would be a point at which a further restriction of a certain operation would not necessarily improve efficiency. One can detect here the fundamental law of diminishing returns, which circumscribes so many economic processes. But manufacture was driven out by the factory system. Under mechanization, new principles of division apply. A man's actions become the operations of a machine. 'Possibilities were now present that were never feasible before' (Clark, 1975, 9). One of these aroused the anger of the Scotsman Ludd, who enjoined the workers to smash the machines, which were more efficient partly because they made labour superfluous. Anyone who wishes to curtail the development of technology is really a Luddite, though a soft-line one if he leaves existing technology intact and merely demands a ban on new technology.

Unemployment as a side effect of technical progress has been a preoccupation of the theorists for a long time. Many a theory of crisis has been built around it, since, as purchasing power falls as a result of unemployment, the markets for the recently increased production will shrink. Say's 'law of demand' has given comfort since 1803, for as long as it operates a balance is assured. The modern economist who still accepts it, stresses compensatory mechanisms: an increased level of investment in labour-saving machinery in one firm will bring new business to another, the supplier; or to a third firm, for whom the end-product of recently mechanized production will mean cheaper raw material; or to the engineering industry, where new orders come in as a result of mechanization. Labour that has become superfluous where technological advance strikes may be much in demand elsewhere in the industrial complex. And since different techniques develop asynchronically and occur in different branches of industry at different times, it is even possible for shortages of manpower to occur, in which case migrant labour has to be recruited. The theoreticians of compensation seem to be proven right, and anyway Say thought that the mechanization process would slow down gradually as it became increasingly difficult to think up new inventions.

This view has been exploded; as mentioned above, new industrial techniques often arise out of the combination of older techniques - and as the number of techniques expand, so does the range of possibilities for combination. Seen in this way, it is a process which will by nature never stagnate but accelerate. And to the extent that it becomes economical, in the face of rising wages, to introduce machines and equipment aimed at labour substitution, the theoreticians of expulsion are proven right: total investment must progressively increase if redundant labour is to be absorbed elsewhere in the economy.

Moreover, the labour factor is of course not as homogeneous or as mobile as the compensation theory conveniently assumes. The service sector, which is less conducive to this kind of substitution and hence in the advanced countries has absorbed much of the released industrial labour, eventually also is subject to a finite demand. Unemployment rises relentlessly, and purchasing power has to be supplemented out of budget deficits: stagflation has arrived, the exact opposite of what the Keynesian mechanisms for the stimulation of the economy should have achieved. Supporters of harmony, simplicity and organic growth here rightly shake their heads, but the same process also included elements to their liking. For besides economies of labour there are also economies of natural resources. Technological development has been partly aimed at reducing relative capital inputs, or for that matter all other inputs. (In absolute terms capital inputs have of course risen due to the expansion of consumption.) Kaldor rejoiced: 'There is no question from every point of view of the superiority of the latest and more capitalistic technologies' (Stewart and Streeten, 1971, 148). A technique which leads to the same product, but uses greater quantities of a certain factor of production - an older technique therefore - is classed as inferior; and whatever is considered superior now will gradually lose that predicate as technology advances. Innovation is then called 'capital-saving', and the extent to which development is steered in this direction depends on the price of capital.

A second set of correlations is revealed: rising wages give rise to labour-saving devices, and expensive capital gives rise to capital-saving devices. It is now clear that technological innovation, far from being autonomous, is introduced on the basis of economic considerations. There was a severe shortage of labour in the nineteenth-century United States, and Habakkuk has shown that at that time predominantly labour-saving techniques were developed (1976). The theory is backed up by empirical evidence, and authors like Harrod, Hicks and Solow have discussed the phenomena in great detail. The subject will not be dealt with further here, but it should be mentioned that Abramovitz, who has studied the causes of the rise of income in the United States in the periods 1869-79 and 1944-53, comes to the surprising conclusion that the mere rise of capital inputs cannot explain fully the manifold increase in output per head during these periods. This finding has fanned interest in technological progress and hence in changes in the nature of this factor. It has also produced the dichotomy embodied/disembodied: changes which are embodied in capital goods and as such represent technical advance, and the improvement of the organization of production and training of labour which also contribute to expansion. The unexplained residue of historical-statistical study, elegantly coined our 'ignorance coefficient', has latterly revived interest in the old issue of the division of labour among countries and the resultant trade flows. Ever since Ricardo these have been explained in terms of the relative natural advantage which every country is supposed to enjoy in the production of certain goods.

Now that the influence of natural circumstances has waned, there is a tendency to explain the world division of labour in terms of technology. The prevailing notion at present is that the technical manufacture of a product passes through a number of cycles during which comparative advantage is transferred from one country to another. The first impulse is found in a technologically advanced country, where the industry which first applies the innovation not only possesses highly developed skills itself, but also has access to the supply and services sectors where the skills reside to remedy any teething troubles.

Subsequently, the imitation phase as observed by Schumpeter occurs. A technique is standardized and adopted by other firms; and other countries where technology is not as advanced gain access to it. In the last phase, referred to as 'maturity', the industrially backward countries are offered a slice of the cake. All technical and organizational obstacles have been overcome, and a 'turnkey' factory can be set up almost anywhere.

Lagging behind, keeping pace, catching up, and being in the vanguard are thus all reduced to cycles in the manufacture of technically new, older and obsolete goods. The problem of economic underdevelopment emerges following a theoretical reflection on the role of technology in the growth process.

Technology destroys jobs but also creates jobs.

New machines relegate older machines to the scrap-heap, but their products are available to a wider section of the population: income rises, the economy expands.

But technology is more than that which is produced; as

knowledge and a way of life it is present in the minds of those who design and use it. All members of industrial society are affected by it every day. Yet the social sciences still have not come to grips with it.

5 The temptations of economies of scale

> 'We, development economists, persuaded the developing countries that life begins at $1,000.' (Mahbub el Haq)

It may be true that the world has been opened up by modern means of transport and communication, but in the past people also travelled to other continents. Europeans have been visiting tropical areas for centuries, and observed for instance that the natives had very big feet (Berliner, 1962). The old journals now seem amusing, because our knowledge of the outside world is greater. We know that the tropical forest is inhabited by animals with long trunks, because we have seen elephants in the zoo. Nature programmes on television document an even stranger fauna. We are, as the contemporary term has it, 'informed', also, about the people living in these exotic places; Oxfam, Third World First and Voluntary Service Overseas see to that.

Even before the communications explosion our countries were occasionally visited by people from far-away places. What impressions did these visitors gain of our Western society? There is a tale of a Malay villager who was taken to a Western city and whose reactions were recorded - an early experiment in cross-cultural contact. When on his return to his village he was asked what had struck him most, he said: that one man could carry so many bananas! What he had remembered of the bustle of the metropolis was a fruit vendor with a handcart. The phenomenologist who hears this anecdote will have little difficulty with the interpretation: man recognizes in his environment only that which he can place in a meaningful context. The villager was familiar with the transport of bananas, he had seen enough people toiling with them at home. He had never seen them on a cart, because carts were not part of his material culture. The starting point for the novel means of transport for him was the banana; the wheel, crucial to this technology, he had not even noticed, could not have noticed, because he could not relate it to anything in his experience.

However much the field of experience of many people has broadened - so that now we are beginning to see ourselves not without satisfaction as citizens of the world - we still are most saturated with our own culture. This is still our first frame of reference. An economist or technician travelling around in a developing country encounters a deviant system of subsistence and a different technology. All this is alien to his own frame of reference. The goal of the trip is not to record the immediately obvious (that the natives have big feet) but to evaluate what he sees from the point of view of development. As an expert in a developing area he applies standards of efficiency. What he finds is therefore condemned in advance, for it falls short as a wealth-generating system. The country is poor, and it must be assisted in overcoming its poverty. Even if the Western observer puts aside all personal interest, forgets the fact that his Institute would like to set up a project, that his firm would like to sell certain machines, and that his education and training have prepared him for an economic system where such institutes and machines have a place - he would still be incapable of judging what he finds as anything else but inappropriate. It has been shown to be inappropriate, for otherwise the country would have been developed and the expert advice unnecessary. His advice is unequivocal: replace the means and mode of production with those which industrial society has produced and which have created great wealth there.

THE GERIATRIC ECONOMY

Although the theory of product cycles provides a satisfactory explanation of the trade flows between the developed countries of the world, its relevance to countries where industries have been established only recently is less obvious. 'The Economist' is too rash when it rejects subsidies to British companies to protect employment on the grounds that they are the industries of yesterday: 'tomorrow these are all going to the South Koreas' (4 March 1978, 9). The quasi-monopoly of the new but already obsolete product is maintained under its brand name longer than warranted for technical reasons. A kind of geriatric strategy, wholly responsible in terms of industrial organization, prevents the shift that theory predicts. Instead, a production which has not reached the maturity phase can still be transferred to a developing country either to avoid import restrictions there, or to underpin a defensive management policy which aims to keep ahead of the competition.

The situation becomes more opaque in the case of a transfer of part of the production process, namely the labour-intensive operations, to a developing country. In all the cases mentioned here, distortions arise in the distribution expected on the basis of the product cycle theory. Proponents of the centre-periphery model will recognize without difficulty that this is explained by the fact that the main investment decisions are taken in the centre.

It is, however, clear from the product cycle that what at one point is construed as progress can at the same time, or somewhat later, be regression. Or to put it in another way: in the economy, growth leads to obsolescence. This is true in the industrialized countries, where manufacturers of horse harnesses and whips, of coal and then oil heaters, of oil and then gas lamps, have lost out against the new substitutes. Thus, train and bus come off second best against the motor car, the ocean liner against the aeroplane, the cinema against television. New products are brought on the market because it has become technically possible and because the dramatic rise in incomes, partly the outcome of this process, guarantees a market. The same happens when an industry settles in a developing country, except that the shock is greater because the gap between the traditional and imported technology is that much wider. To mourn the demise of batiks, spinning and weaving is understandable, but if the materials, clothes and furniture supplied by the new factory are cheaper and thus brought within the reach of a larger section of consumers, then this is beneficial. It is precisely this benefit that a development strategy strives for. This is what happened in the phase of industrialization in the rich countries, and this is what should happen in the poor countries as well. That in any case was the view defended in the 1950s by leading lights of growth theory like Galenson and Leibenstein (1955, 370). The same process had guided the industrialized countries to a level of wealth which even the most optimistic forecasts had not thought possible. The scale of productive activities became ever larger. Rising profits were invested in new and improved machinery; innovation seemed to become the norm. In Britain, where progress along this road was rather hesitant, firms with more than 1500 employees accounted for 27 per cent of all jobs in

1958; they comprised only 15 per cent in 1935 (Stewart, 1974, 20). Economies of scale cut unit costs. As competition compelled firms to pass on the savings in the selling price of goods, real wages were increased.

Lastly, it should be noted that larger firms especially prospered, because they were in a position to finance their own research into the technological improvements on which the whole miracle was based.

Against this background, the categorical assertion of the inherent superiority of the capitalist mode of production becomes almost persuasive. Even economists of the opposite camp arrive at parallel conclusions: Drobyshev has argued that the advantages accruing from the law of the Disadvantage of the Early Start are becoming greater - that is, the gap between the wealthy and the poor is closing - as the latest machinery is employed and the frustrating stages of transition are bypassed (1974, 217). In some countries and in some respects the strategy could be deemed a success. For instance, in 1968 an ILO report found the degree of mechanization of Colombia equal to that of the earlier starters Spain and Greece. Investment per worker in the Latin American textile industry rose from the base of 100 for 1950 to 190 in 1960 and 310 in 1965 (Stewart, 1977, 84).

Industrial production widens the scope for standardization, by which more operations are simplified. So it was found that a building brick was more uniform and of better quality if the cement mixture had been mixed mechanically rather than manually. Even in the field of transport, which is still a labour-intensive sector in the industrialized countries as well, mechanization sometimes presents an advantage, because damage can be reduced (Stewart, 1974, 26). Indeed, some goods cannot be manufactured at all without the use of machines: in the petrochemical and aluminium industries technology rules, and only a few minor operations are performed by hand. The same applies to a greater or lesser extent to many consumer goods. It could be said, with slight exaggeration, that modernization cannot be achieved without capital-intensive production. If we want to build houses and prevent their sudden collapse, it is advisable to prepare the cement mechanically. If we want to wear Western-style shirts, this choice is reflected in the weaving and spinning process, even in the cotton production at source. How much industrialists are preoccupied with quality control - properly exercised only in industrial production - can be gathered from a study commissioned in Brazil, where managers, asked to assess the importance of different factors of production, put the product quality top of the list, even above the size of the market or wage costs (Morley and Smith, 1974, 239). This reflects the awareness of the consumers' 'modern' demands. But a conservative purchaser who prefers the quality of the traditional production method does not necessarily appreciate uniformity. In Indonesia smokers rejected the smooth, machine-rolled cigarette and continued to prefer the hand-rolled, conical traditional product (Timmer et al., 1975, 78). Though an instructive instance, this behaviour pattern is not decisive.

Sales of a product will be hampered much more seriously by a lack of purchasing power in the economy. The advocates of large-scale technology expect improvement in this respect in the long run, the historical development of the European economies being cited as the precedent. Not many jobs will be created directly by investment in advanced technology - this is not one of its objectives - but the prospects of self-financing will improve markedly if productive capacity is organized on a larger scale; and investment-intensive development programmes will in the long run generate more income. Proponents of this view acquiesce in the initially skewed distribution of incomes, and indeed it is not wholly calamitous: the ratio of saving may be increased and future investment thus assured. It is profits that are the great source of finance; wages are mainly for immediate consumption. An extreme version of this line recommends the introduction of the latest available techniques quite independently of the wage rates level (Harris and Todaro, 1970).

THE MIGRATING ECONOMY

Although foreign investors are often eager to calculate their returns on the basis of the low wages obtaining in the developing countries, they also occasionally betray an ethnocentric belief that job performance cannot possibly be satisfactory at such a low wage. In a feasibility study, an American industrialist in Indonesia simply carried over American wage rates: 'You get what you pay for in productivity', he explained (Timmer et al., 1975, 84). The Nederlands Economisch Instituut approached the matter rather more subtly. In a cost analysis three types of lathe, with an increasing degree of labour-intensity, were compared in situations then characteristic of a developed country (hourly wage $ 1.50 and interest 4 per cent) and an underdeveloped country (hourly wage $ 0.05 and interest 15 per cent). Unit costs are of course partly influenced by projected sales. At 150 units of production the simplest machines yielded the same cost price in both situations. The more mechanized lathe was found to be more efficient for a developed country at sales of 150 to 750 units, but in the underdeveloped country greater efficiency was reached only at 1,000 units. From 2,800 units the choice fell on the automated lathe in the developed country, and for the underdeveloped country this was considered economic at 3,600 units. It is noteworthy that the spread is less wide than might be expected considering the disparity in wage costs. This is because, firstly, the investment in the more automated machines is substantial and, secondly, the interest rate is high. In subsequent studies, which will be discussed below, doubts have been raised regarding the last point (NEI, 1957, 33).

Many Eastern European economists are also partial to large-scale development. They prescribe an initial build-up of heavy industry, on the grounds that it lays the foundation for the mass manufacture of consumer goods. The strategy does require the labour force to make considerable sacrifices for a long period of time. This aspect is treated rather lightly at central planning levels, perhaps because paradise is thought to be around the corner - and of course it would appear first in the seats of government and embrace the planners themselves.

Supporters of the development strategy of rapid industrialization will recognise that modern production processes are alien to the economies on which they are to be grafted. But in their view this is precisely the cause of their underdevelopment. In order for the backward economies to catch up, these differences, which have the character of obstacles, must be removed forthwith through industrialization. Such a programme refuses to acknowledge differences in climate, availability of resources, and infrastructure between the one hundred or so underdeveloped countries, and prescribes a simple, universal remedy: build factories of the newest type, and all will be well. Many development experts must have thought Julius Nyerere a spoilsport when he said: 'We aren't ready for the tractor, either financially or technically, but we are ready for the ox-plough' (Heierli, 1976, 50). Precisely on this point economists and technicians had concurred. Both are motivated by a Veblenian 'instinct of workmanship' or a Schumpeterian 'half-artistic joy in technically perfecting'; both share a preference for the larger, more developed industrial unity which increases both labour and capital productivity. The reasons for this preference are of course obvious, for these experts have grown up and have been educated in an industrial climate in which these criteria are constantly applied.

Solicited advice by economists and engineers to a firm or (until recently) a government authority is not given with considerations of employment creation or income distribution, let alone 'basic needs' in mind: the question whether the commodity is deemed worthy of being added to the existing range already on the market does not arise.

A psychologist has noted that when people migrate from one culture to another they tend to carry with them the technologies they have learned and try to apply them unchanged in the new environment (McClelland, 1969, 86). And indeed Pickett et al. found that the experts who designed the sugar cane refineries in Ethiopia and the shoe factories in Ghana, being oblivious of the enormous discrepancies in factor prices, had designed and set up variants of the most advanced technologies from Europe (1974, 47). Local industrialists will readily accept the introduction of the newest technology; the more modern the better. Wells observed in Indonesia that managers rated mechanization and automation favourably, even though it might force up their cost prices. The manager of a factory which produced hand-rolled cigarettes gave the opinion that an automatic plant, for which the unit cost price would undoubtedly rise due to the high rate of interest, would be a profitable investment 'in the long run'. A rival firm with greater financial resources indeed had already ordered automatic machines without apparently considering the effect on costs. In similar cases the desire to produce a high-quality product or resolve personnel management problems were often mentioned as justifications for capital-intensive investment. Occasionally, to use Keynes's phrase, an industrialist showed himself a defunct economist's disciple, this time in reference to Schumpeter: 'You have to modernize to stay ahead of the competition' (Timmer et al., 1975, 75).

THE RECIPIENT ECONOMY

Financial aid donated by the rich countries also acts as a strong impulse for large-scale development projects. This is unavoidable when funds are transferred with the proviso that they must be spent in the donor country. The Dutch government, fairly typical in this respect, published under the progressive-sounding title 'The job of job-creation', a document recommending active state participation in the investment decisions of developing countries; 'In particular this could be done by expanding the facilities for so-called turn-key projects' (1977, 91). In this form of aid, a company in the donor country is commissioned to carry out a whole project, using its own expertise, materials and equipment. The arrangement is intended to prevent transferred funds from being spent outside the donor country. Under these circumstances, 'aid' will boost the donor economy and will have no adverse effects on its balance of payments. Now there is no need to carry international aid policy to the extreme of striving for the masochistic opposite, but for the present purpose the system's drawbacks are shown clearly in the end result which is a modern, highly automated 'turnkey' plant. And even if the (European) contractor is full of good intentions - and why shouldn't he be once the order has been booked? - his efforts to render optimal services to the recipient country will be determined by the specific knowledge and skills at its disposal. Within its field of experience, a European or American firm is unlikely to carry out its task according to criteria of employment creation and income redistribution in the recipient economy.

In Thailand, roads were built with funds obtained under aid schemes with the above strings attached. Road construction offers an excellent opportunity for a labour-intensive approach. But in this case a highly capital-intensive method was followed. It improved the country's infrastructure but failed to produce the spin-offs which are crucial to get the economy off the ground. It is evident that, since purchasing power expands with the creation of employment, local business will benefit from a potential rise in demand. What is more, the supply of raw materials and tools has an accelerating effect at various levels of economic activity. If modern techniques are embodied in the project, technical capacities will be called upon which local industry cannot provide. What Hirschman has called backward 'linkage' then fails to occur. And linkage with other sectors of the economy also becomes more tenuous. Hoogvelt's discovery that the Rhodesian economy was anything but damaged by the sanctions imposed after 1965, that on the contrary it was stimulated, is explained by the enhanced internal linkage following the blockade (Hoogvelt and Child, 1973, 41ff.).

The opportunity to study these effects arose in west Pakistan, where a comparison could be made between government-sponsored wells drilled with modern technology and private wells struck on a small scale. In the latter a labour-intensive technology was employed, and it turned out that local workshops which supplied the necessary tools experienced a strong upturn in business (Johnston, 1967, 394).

THE CORRUPTED ECONOMY

Government representatives of developing countries often still opt for capital-intensive technologies, even though there is now ample evidence to show that this type of technology is not necessarily the best. Their inclination to give priority to personal aggrandizement plays a not unimportant part here. The Lockheed affair has shown that the big European and American corporations at times resort to offering attractive bonuses to those who are in a position to influence investment decisions in their favour. And there is no reason to assume that the intervention of prominent persons in the awarding of contracts is confined to the aircraft industry. Some observers have also noted that civil servants sometimes resign, only to accept a comfortable post with a firm that, on their advice, has been allowed to build plants in their country (Neersø, 1975, 50). Such machinations transform an untied loan into a tied one, and the resultant agreements may have but little bearing on the economic interests of the recipient country as a whole.

Even a joint venture intended to support local enterprise, whose performance will depend on the technology adopted, does not guarantee a rational choice of technology. The interests of the foreign partner - note that their revenue is generated elsewhere - probably dictate the abandonment of economic rationality by the local partner. It is again not inconceivable that the prospect of personal financial gain will induce the latter to betray his firm's true interests. But even if industrialists in the poor country have no association with any form of foreign aid, it is still possible for their personal gain to be independent of, or even opposed to, the interest of the enterprise. In the majority of developing countries the official exchange rate does not reflect the actual purchasing power of the currency. The industrialist who is granted a licence to buy machines from abroad, pays for them in his own overvalued currency; consequently he buys the equipment at a price considerably below its real value. Such price distortion makes a level of capital expenditure acceptable in economic terms that would normally put a severe strain on production costs.

During a study of these practices in Pakistan researchers encountered in addition the phenomenon of the inflated invoice. After the local industrialist has obtained his import licence he arranges with the foreign supplier to sell him equipment at a fictitious invoice price, higher than he actually pays. After remittance, the portion that represents overpayment is deposited by the supplier into a foreign bank account of the local industrialist, who can then dispose of the money for personal use. If he wishes to change it back into his own currency, he will be able to do so in the free market at a rate two or three times the official rate. The gains realized in this manner render irrelevant all the investment considerations applied under more beseeming circumstances (Winston, 1971, 321). The industrialist thus making a handsome profit will try to expand and modernize his plant even if he has only a limited use for the imported capital equipment. He will cultivate political contacts to dissuade the government from such policies as devaluation or the lifting of exchange controls. Furthermore, he will invariably choose the most expensive, and hence the least labour-intensive, capital equipment; and if at all possible he will write it off almost immediately and then apply for a new import licence to replace it. Winston has estimated that such a transaction could realize an instant profit of 25 per cent on the sum invested.

THE EXPORTING ECONOMY

For the export of goods the reverse trade practice is profitable. Indian firms, for instance, have been known to use under-invoicing, so that a surplus of foreign currency is obtained for personal purposes. Although the Indian government demands of firms that they finance their capital investments out of the foreign currency yields on their exports, the facts show a rather different picture: between 1961 and 1966 exports accounted for only 2.9 per cent of the aggregate business transactions of these firms, while for raw materials and for technical equipment 15.5 and 1.6 per cent, respectively, of turnover was imported (Neersø, 1975, 48).

It should be mentioned here that for a long time development experts advocated an active export strategy, which was expected to act as a strong impulse to development.

Export orientation was recommended as the 'spearhead of development'. The term 'outward-looking policy' was also liberally used to indicate that all parochialism had been transcended. It was not so much primary goods that were considered here, for it was clear that if tropical countries could produce them in surplus, and therefore enjoy the 'comparative advantage' of classical theory, then the drive for exchange could easily misfire. On the world market prices of primary goods fell relatively to finished products. Thus there was a real danger that the exports of the poor countries would yield diminishing quantities of the products their rich trading partners offered them in exchange. Moreover, primary production is definitely not the activity which will stimulate business in the country of origin. And, lastly, governments of countries which had only recently achieved their political independence understandably shied away from a strategy which would prolong and even increase their economic dependence.

According to the Heckscher-Ohlin-Samuelson version of the familiar Ricardian views hinted at just now, a country which possesses a certain factor of production in abundance should exploit it so as to gain an advantage in international trade. Since the developing countries have a plethora of labour, they should concentrate on producing labour-intensively for export. In the 1960s this policy was put into practice in South Korea, Taiwan, Hong Kong and Singapore - all countries with minimal natural resources, so in fact they had little choice. All four succeeded in their objective: in record years South Korea's industrial exports rose by 35 per cent and employment by 13 per cent. Some foreign corporations draw their conclusions from the wage-cost analyses they have commissioned for different regions of the world. They choose to transfer the labour-intensive part of their production process to the low-wage countries. This practice is most advanced in the electronics industry. Because the products are imported at an early stage of manufacture and are sent back after certain operations have been carried out, the boost to the balance of payments need not be considerable: it is restricted to the value added. It follows from this interlocking of production into a supranational industrial complex that the successful export strategy tends to reside in the technically more advanced sphere. If one hopes to compete in this field, development along capital-intensive lines is imperative; it is already required in order to meet the demands of quality and standardization made in the countries where industrial products are to be sold. An incidental fashion may fleetingly create a demand for a certain cottage industry product, but to erect a development policy on such a fad would be foolish. Even if quality is improved by technical perfection there is the problem of mistrust, which Japan had to contend with for years and which is now directed against India. 'Even when Indian goods are of high quality, the generally bad reputation of Indian goods means that they can normally only be sold in the international market if they are about 20% cheaper than similar goods produced in developed countries' (Neersø, 1975, 47).

Prebisch, Schiavo-Campo, Singer and others have commented on the gradual switch-over of the export industries to more capital-intensive production methods. The technical expertise and equipment required are imported from the industrial countries. And so the circle leading to large-scale production has been completed.

THE IMPORTING ECONOMY

A development strategy which takes the balance of payments as a point of departure, but considers only its passive side, is that of the so-called import substitution. The idea is simple. The objective of industrialization is the production of industrial goods. They are imported from the rich countries and sold to the more affluent domestic consumers. An analysis of this market yields information about the sales turnover of the different products; among them there will undoubtedly be some for which demand is so strong that manufacture in the country itself will be profitable. Arrangements are made to produce the popular goods locally, while at the same time the importation of competing foreign products is prohibited or counteracted by duties. The policy is justified to free enterprise buffs by pointing to the longer-term interests that are thus served. This is the same 'infant industry argument' once used by the historicist school to defend the measures taken to foster an indigenous German industrial base and to protect it from British imports! At issue was then, and is now, how far the national economy actually suffers as a result of the inevitably higher cost of local production. For previously the consumer could buy the imported equivalents at a lower price. To this objection it is retorted that in the long run local production will be able to compete successfully, in terms of price and quality, against the imported goods. The country is then better off with its own industry.

But this applies only if during the time of protection granted to them, the national industries succeed in organizing production so that they can pit themselves against foreign competition when the trade barriers are lifted. It is not clear whether in the absence of constant price and quality comparisons - typical of the vacuum - the temptation to throw considerations of cost-efficiency overboard can be resisted; and whether at the end of a period of protection the temptation to request an extension will not override the willingness to face competition. All this is familiar from the history of industrialization in Europe, yet those who strive for economic independence apparently cast all doubts aside. The higher cost of home-produced goods represents the price to be paid for that independence - some sacrifices will have to be made to establish a domestic industry.

A more detailed study of the actual ramification of the strategy, which has been pursued for years in Latin American countries in particular, brings other objections to light. As we saw, in the period of free imports, the industrial goods were sold primarily to the consumers with greater purchasing power. These are traditionally concentrated in the urban areas, where spending patterns are influenced by, if not based on, the Western model. Much has been written in development literature about the so-called demonstration effect. A concept in fact borrowed from Duesenberry's explanation of consumer behaviour in Western industrial society, it represents the emulation of higher by lower income brackets. It has been well documented, although interpreted differently: for Veblen it was an irritant when it eroded ideals of equality and thrift, while for Schumpeter it was a boon when consumer desire stimulated production. Nurkse applied the demonstration effect to the desire for consumer goods fanned by examples from abroad, but he was in fact anticipated here by Hume, who again saw it as a beneficial force: 'the chief advantage which arises from commerce with strangers. It rouses men from their indolence ... raises in them a desire for a more splendid way of life' (Rosenberg, 1976, 90).

But of course people can only satisfy those needs if, as a spin-off from the industrialization process, their incomes rise to pay for the goods on offer. And as we will see below, this is by no means assured in the strategy of import substitution. Critical observers - and there is no scarcity of this commodity - point out that consumer aspirations are expressed above all in the 'centre', in the big city, where the rich indulge themselves while the poor look on. But widespread migration to the cities indicates that in the countryside, too, the potential consumer has woken up to the new age of desire. Duvignaud describes a Tunisian village in which economically, technologically and politically nothing has changed, except that the children learn to read and write. Ex-soldiers tell stories of what they have seen in the modern outside world, while the government completes the picture through radio broadcasts. Nothing has changed, the villagers have seen nothing different with their own eyes, but their expectations have risen to the point where they nearly rebelled (1970). The same is reported from India, where Gandhi was once put foward as a shining example of simplicity (Alvares, 1975). In Indonesia certain material facilities are considered modern, and in virtue of their modernity they are thought desirable (Quarles van Ufford, 1976, 724).

On the Caribbean island of Curaçao, where there are as many cars registered as there are families, the oil company was induced to run an advertising campaign on television urging people to tank up more than a few litres at a time - apparently such a large percentage of the family budget was spent on the car that not enough was left over to pay for the essential complement, petrol (Duller, 1975, 33). The motor car is everywhere *the* ostentation of achieved wealth. Fiat prided itself in adverts on the fact that the customer could stay with the company all his life as he climbed the social ladder, by trading in his 500 model for a 600, 1000 and 1500 model. 'L'homme', Rullière noted aptly, 's'évalue à la cylindrée' (1971, 175). And where the car cannot penetrate, the symbolic function of indicating achieved status is taken over by other means of transport: the scooter on the mud tracks of Bali, and the outboard motor in the jungles of Surinam.

Advertising, inseparable companion to industrial consumption, also reaches these out-of-the-way places. In its area of origin, Europe and the United States, one can just about argue convincingly that advertising does not so much create new demands as differentiate existing ones (Brooks, 1973, 253). In the poor countries, advertising acts as a source of information; without it (potential) consumers would know less about the world around them. Yet it is unlikely that they will be able to participate in the good life as promised by the advertising industry. For the goods concerned are the outcome of production processes which have been developed in the industrial countries. Radios and television sets, electrical appliances and all the other wonderful goodies being extolled in the media are manufactured in factories stocked with highly expensive capital-intensive machinery imported from the industrial countries. Import substitution promotes a technology ill suited to existing scarcities; what is more, it creates only a few jobs. Morawetz has calculated that a 100 million dollar investment in the import-substituting Colombian petrochemical industry created only 2,500 jobs, while the same sum invested in labour-intensive industries would have created 50,000 jobs. What a difference this would have made for the country becomes clear when one knows that the total employment in firms of five or more staff in Colombian manufacturing industry is only about 350,000 (Morawetz, 1974, 510). A distribution of income which was unequal, and hence supported the initial demand for the goods to be substituted with purchasing power, does not become any more equal through the strategy of import substitution. Barnett therefore dismisses this development policy as a failure. But in the light of the above discussion it is difficult to accept his conclusion that an export-oriented policy should replace it (1974, 13).

THE PATENTED ECONOMY

The cost to poor countries of adopting an industrial production process is not exhausted by the purchase of the machines required. The processes are in private industrial ownership and are protected by patents. Patent laws date from an age when the transfer of technology to non-industrialized countries had not even been contemplated. They were supposed to assure the inventor of the fruits of his own inventiveness, at least for a limited period. Without them, unrestricted copying by competitors would negate any advantage gained, and all incentives to innovation would be lost. Also, because considerable sums have been invested in the research and development phase which precedes the marketing of the product, it is acceptable that the firm which took the risk when the outcome was still in doubt, is protected against imitation once the product is marketable. The right to exploit an invention, or instead demand payment from third parties, is laid down in a patent. Interested parties may apply to the inventor for a manufacturing license against payment of royalties. International protection is regulated by the Paris Convention of 1883, which has been revised several times, but not since the developing countries have gained their independence and could press any demands. Of the eighty member countries of the International Union for the Protection of Industrial Property in 1973, forty-four were developing countries. That may seem quite a large proportion, but it should be borne in mind that the other sixty-odd developing countries represent 80 per cent of the world's population (NAR, 1977, 22). Meanwhile UNCTAD has been studying the problem; new guidelines are being drafted to protect more effectively the interests of the poor countries. For it is undeniable that the Paris Convention, in so far as it assumes that royalty payments between countries will tend to even out, is out of touch with the present situation. The contributions of the advanced industrial countries to the growth of knowledge in production exceed by far what for the time being (or perhaps for ever) the developing countries can be expected to contribute. When theoreticians express with confidence that alternately different countries will set the technological pace, they evidently do not allow for the possibility or even probability of some countries lagging behind permanently (Williams, 1973, 21).

It is of course the poor countries that lag behind. They contribute to the payments without receiving compensation in the form of transfer of technology: of the approximately 3.5 million patents in existence today, only some 200,000 have been granted in developing countries, but for 84 per cent of them the patentees are foreign companies, and only 5 to 10 per cent of them are actually used in the developing countries (NAR, 1977, 4). In contrast, it was estimated in 1965 that payments of the Third World amounted to $ 100 million; in 1980 this figure was probably around $ 400 million. This includes not only the direct reimbursements for the use of technology protected by patents, but also all other payments for licenses, the use of brand names, and training. The dependence is so great that even without the protection provided by patents it would be difficult for infant industrial countries, with their limited supply of skilled labour, to set up a complicated production process. Since it is not always easy to enforce observance of patent rights once industrial equipment has been delivered and installed, foreign investors sometimes purposely transfer complex machines which are difficult to copy; and if the investor withdraws, the local staff left to its own devices will not be able to operate and maintain the machine ('The Economist', 31 December 1977, 22).

THE MULTINATIONALIZED ECONOMY

Such perfidy is only to be expected from multinationals - a social-economic category which has altogether fallen into disgrace. The aversion to industry and commerce, temporarily forgotten (even by the left) in the period of economic recovery after the war, is now again widespread. The concept of harmony, which in the post-war euphoria caused European trade union leaders to put peaceful industrial relations before income redistribution, has been abandoned. The opposition of interests between employers and employees, both members of the motorized public and rivals in the search for the elusive parking space rather than anything else, has again been underpinned philosophically with theories of conflict. The distribution of the increasing wealth has again become a bone of contention. Workers who for quite a while had been 'employees' have again become the proletariat, and the capitalists are hated with new venom.

Concern about the environment nourished the dislike of big business, which was seen as the great polluter and the violator of nature. The concept of alienation was brought back into circulation, the concern about man's non-material needs was reawakened.

There was not much talk of productivity any more, for the product was superfluous, even actually harmful. If the detergents in the washing powder did not poison the housewife, they certainly killed the fish. Every study of environmental pollution made reference to Lake Erie, which in the 1960s was branded as a 'dead' lake: it had died as a result of our ecological sins. Commoner wrote a funeral oration entitled 'The Killing of a Great Lake'; so did Bronner: 'When Lake Erie started to die it went in twelve years'. Not informed about catch figures, which towards the end of the 1960s reached record levels, the government banned the use of phosphates in detergents. The substitute, however, also presented problems. The most widely used one was banned in 1970. So washing powders again contained phosphates. In the meantime a technical process had been developed to remove phosphates from effluent. But to build the new installations would cost time and money, money from public funds - a politically less attractive proposition. However, the authorities had another line of attack at their disposal: there were only three big producers of the objectionable product, and they had to be dealt with. A party could make political capital out of an anti-monopoly campaign. 'Big corporations ... were suddenly back in fashion as public enemies' (Fleming, 1972, 50). What matters here are not the merits and demerits of this piece of ecological history. The water-purification installations did get built; Colgate-Palmolive, Lever Brothers and Proctor and Gamble did survive the assault. But in this atmosphere of accusation the big corporations were found guilty without trial.

In the 1930s, the economic crisis aroused a similar unease in (industrial) culture. It found concrete shape in the dogma of imperfect competition. The many curves and graphs published at the time still exhibited the states of equilibrium which had been the traditional fare of economics, but they were shifted along the axes, plotted in a less favourable line. The corporations meanwhile have grown even larger and - like everybody else, have profited from the improvements in transport and communications - extending their operations beyond national frontiers.

The strong opposition aroused is tainted with nationalistic overtones. In 'Le Défit Americain' Servan-Schreiber spoke out against what he saw as the take-over of French industry by American interests. The English are also far from pleased about Arab investment in their country: the thought that not only the guests but the owners of the Dorchester should be Arabs saddens them, though protests are limited to indignant letters in 'The Times' and 'The Arab Challenge' remains unwritten. In the light of this reaction, the opposition encountered by European and American corporations in the Third World becomes wholly understandable. The theory of imperfect competition might lead one to believe that the monopolist dispenser of technology, who is after all intent on fetching the highest possible price from any demand, would offer the developing countries a reduced price because demand there is more elastic and the monopolist maximization of returns would be better served by higher turnover at lower prices. This belief was still proclaimed in 1970 by the prominent economist Johnson, an interesting instance of the faith that reality mirrors the descriptions in the textbooks (Morley and Smith, 1977, 165). Rather, a majority of observers are of the opinion that corporate management will adopt a strategy that is not only contrary to theory but to all precepts of industry and commerce. It is opined, namely, that the corporations, to which a blind imperialist inspiration is apparently attributed, ignore matters of cost. In this view they invest, preferably on a large scale, but take no account of local labour costs or the rate of interest. From this we can see how a futurologist can dismiss the multinational corporations as 'artifacts of old-think (that will) eventually wither away' (Love, 1977, 79).

Helleiner honestly believes that American managers deciding on investments in countries with notoriously low wage levels pass over this fact on the assumption that labour productivity will be so low as to cancel out the advantages of low wage costs (1975, 168). Wells even found a case in which American wage levels had been used as the basis of feasibility studies for a country with a wage rate well below one dollar per day (1974, 116). Boon, steeped in the economics of technology long before the concept 'adapted' had been invented, writes that in their foreign investments, companies commonly calculate with a uniform rate of interest on capital. Sometimes the cost of capital would not be included at all! And of course: with capital costing little or nothing, the technology minimizing labour costs is always preferable. In this case underutilization of equipment does not enter as a cost factor (1976, 734). The company which holds such peculiar ideas of costing has its own engineering works which, one assumes, it does want to keep fully utilized. The marxist economist Baranson, for whom an industrial strategy leading to collapse must seem less undesirable, reports after a study of fifty multinationals that he noticed little adjustment of chosen technology to locally existing conditions (1972).

My own observations in the Caribbean point to the exact opposite. The management of the Curaçao plant of a big American electronics corporation based its production strategy on what was referred to as a 'spectral cost analysis': costs per unit were reviewed at regular intervals so that changes in the wage level or in labour productivity in each of the countries where the corporation had plants were recorded. The production process was planned such that the most labour-intensive operations were carried out in the countries with the lowest wages. Bruton's pronouncement certainly applies to Curaçao in this case: 'Factor substitutability is alive and well in the developing countries' (1972, 43). Strassman reports a similar state of affairs from Mexico. He compared twenty-two local and fourteen American companies, and observed that the latter made relatively the greater use of the factor labour (1968, 190-4). Mason, who studied fourteen local and fourteen American firms in Mexico and the Philippines, also concludes that the American firms brought their production functions better in line with local conditions (1971). Such studies were also undertaken in Brazil, where it was observed that the multinationals had carefully adapted their production methods to the local factor price relationship (Morley and Smith, 1974, 246-57). Investment per worker was only one-third to one-fourth of that in the United States. Finally, from Kenya the ILO reports that in comparison to local firms the foreign companies operated more labour-intensively (Singer, 1977, 85).

Comparisons of this kind could mean that it is not the multinational but local industry which is characterized by a deployment of capital versus labour that does not tally with existing economic conditions and is contrary to the general economic interest. This point has been raised in the above-mentioned sources. Where research findings differ, we must assume that not all European and American corporations have embraced the same corporate policy.

Those who expected on ideological grounds that the multinationals would ride roughshod over local economic interest, which is served by greater labour-intensity, may find comfort in the suspicion that the low level of wages which tempts the corporations to invest in the first place, enables them to exploit the labour force of those countries. But even that does not always seem to be the case, for in the above studies it is also noted the foreign firms 'consistently pay higher wages than do the domestic enterprises' (Timmer et al., 1975, 73). This phenomenon can be explained by the better position which the firm will occupy in the labour market if it offers slightly higher wages to recruit the often very scarce skilled labour. In addition, the parent company will post abroad managers practised in personnel policies; they will be in a position to supervise work and, given the investment, guarantee optimal labour productivity. There are indications that productivity in the foreign-controlled plants is higher than in the local ones. In the electronics assembly plant in Curaçao referred to above, a very active personnel policy was pursued: workers were divided into groups competing with each other in performance, and prizes were awarded for group job performance. In short, artificial incentives were created. Costs were calculated per unit and compared with other plants. Such methods are not at the disposal of the local firms, although in some countries management courses are now offered.

In Bandung, Java, I was able to attend a course taught by American management consultants and followed by students of the local technical university and by industrialists. The organization of the course was in the hands of the psychologist McClelland, who is known for his theory of 'need of achievement'. For him, if 'achievement motivation' is present within a population, economic development will follow; if it is absent, all projects will be in vain.

The training of managers should hence be directed to improving their 'achievement orientation'. This, it is assumed, will initiate economic development. 'The purpose of these courses is to increase the entrepreneurial spirit and the managerial effectiveness of the participants, by considering the motivation and thinking necessary for effective management, rather than the technical skills' (McClelland, 1969, 44).

McClelland starts from the notion that something of the famous social mechanisms described by Weber - that the rise of capitalism was inspired by religious sentiments - has struck root in the industrial countries and has enabled them to retain their advantage in wealth and prosperity. The ethic, as such, he seems to think, can be imbibed without converting to Protestantism. This is the purpose of these management courses. However, the results of the trial course held in Kakinada and Vellore in India hardly give much cause for optimism. As far as I can see, McClelland's theory has withered to the state of a footnote in the development course syllabus. This decline becomes in fact unavoidable against the background of the present view which sees the poverty of the so-called south as caused by the expansionist drive of the so-called north. The transfer of the cultural traits responsible for this drive must therefore be deemed a diabolical act.

But even if industrialists gladly expose their psyches to the manipulations of this or that psychologist to put them in the proper frame of mind, there still remains a more than nagging doubt whether in this way sufficient managers can be trained quickly enough to effect a significant improvement in staff supervision in the industries of the Third World. Ultimately, judgment on even a less crude version of this offshoot of 'scientific management' must be negative.

It is, however, also doubtful whether the frequently encountered condemnation of foreign activity in underdeveloped economies is wholly justified. The world economy is inextricably interwoven, and the worldwide operations of corporations are an aspect of this. An UNCTAD study of the role of foreign enterprises in developing countries found that their presence could well be of mutual benefit (Streeten and Lall, 1973). But one may wonder whether, and how, these foreign firms can be made serviceable to the transfer and application of adapted technology when they have hitherto neglected to do so of their own accord. 'Given good incentives, there are good reasons for believing that multinational firms will become significant suppliers of more appropriate technology and products' (Helleiner, 1975, 178). It is after all they who possess the skills and the equipment needed to carry out research into appropriate technology.

Furthermore, it is important to ensure that local industry in the poor countries, rather than listen to the advice of representatives of Western engineering firms, begins to pay attention to the less capital-intensive technology which also exists, and, as shown above, has occasionally been applied in their countries by foreign firms.

That the installations now predominantly used by local companies are unsuitable can be gathered from the fact that they are far from fully utilized.

THE UNDERUTILIZED ECONOMY

Quite a lot is known about the phenomenon of underutilization. For west Pakistan Winston reports that only 33 per cent of overall industrial capacity is utilized (1971, 38). For Colombia the figure was found to be 20 per cent (Jacob, 1976, 6). In Chile utilization was estimated at 45 per cent, although this figure is distorted by the 80 per cent capacity utilization of the oil industry: in forestry and electrical manufacture a figure of merely 25 per cent is reached (Luders and Cabero, 1970, 10). UNIDO carried out a study in 1967 in Africa, Asia and Latin America and concluded that excess capacity was a general phenomenon. Utilization rarely rose above 60 per cent, whereas American companies operating there achieved 80 per cent (Jacob, 1976, 6). It seems that local industries have in many cases overinvested, and this has had a detrimental effect on employment: the machines may not have been chosen primarily for their complementary requirements of labour, but they would certainly create more jobs if they were more fully utilized. Millan and Schydlowsky have calculated that if presently existing productive capacity in developing countries were used to the full on all available working days, extensive new employment would be created (1973). If sales turnover were to increase further, a shift system could be introduced (rather than an expansion of capacity): at the same level of investment the number of jobs could thus be doubled or even trebled. There is sufficient reason to assume that the apparent excess capacity is related to the predilection for large-scale plants, which local industrialists are tempted to indulge in for the reasons mentioned earlier. But there are other causes. Because of the indivisibility of certain means of production it is possible that even the smallest available capacity can exceed the demand of a small market. This applies to all infant industry, and has been pinpointed as a typical weakness of capitalist production. Jacob rejects the doctrine of indivisibility as bourgeois-technocratic prattle; in the process of reproduction recommended by Marx there is no excess capacity. If firms fall prey to it, they owe it to their capitalist monopoly position. The literature relates cases, however, where underutilization is caused by the existence of too many competitors. This too Jacob attributes to what she scornfully calls 'a sort of "competition"', which is inherent in the capitalist system (Jacob, 1976, 8-12).

THE IRRATIONAL ECONOMY

Yet another cause for excess capacity to be uncovered is the basic incompetence of management, which with its lack of knowledge and experience is allegedly not able to control the production process sufficiently to ensure optimal capacity utilization. There is the additional drawback that an enterprise set up along modern lines in an otherwise traditional economy is soon beset by supply problems, because outside of the modern sector people are not accustomed to producing a constant flow of goods at a consistent quality.

When using the term 'traditional economy' in this context, one should define more precisely: that part of the dual economy which is not, or not yet, organized on the principle of rationality and which therefore does not respond to the incentives offered in an ideal-typical manner by *homo oeconomicus*, '... un être agissant toujours de manière parfaitement rationelle' (Rullière, 1971, 128). In the not particularly refined psychology in which economic theory puts its trust, the concept of incentives or stimuli corresponds roughly to the behavioural experiments with the chicken: when she pecks to the left she is given an electric shock, when she pecks to the right she is given a grain of wheat. In the market economy the principle of exchange rules, and the negative incentive (loss) and the positive (gain or profit) are expressed in money terms. An industrialist who fails to take advantage of a chance to make profits is acting irrationally.

The market system confronts all participants in the economic process with prices; consumers demand goods but also offer labour. Consumers express their preference by using the money they have earned to buy certain goods at certain prices and not to buy others, or at least fewer of those. The goods for which there is a demand will offer healthy profit margins, and for this reason the industrialist will produce them. As the demand for labour rises, the wage sum will rise; and if the supply of labour is exhausted, the resultant scarcity will continue to push up wages. Rises in income lead to a shift in demand for other goods; and supply will in turn react to this. The description of the process presupposes a fully free market economy: it is therefore only an adumbration of what happens in economic reality. When some of the hypotheses are discarded, as has already been done in the theory of imperfect competition, reality is approximated more closely. But it is always assumed that the economic subjects will react to prices, increasing their efforts when a price rises, so that the grains of wheat grow more plentiful and the electric shocks cease.

Economists, it's plain to see
All think that prices are the key
Markets and competition now
Must be the hand that feeds the plow (Edel, 1970, 28)

As with the chicken, this is a case of learned behaviour. In Western society this behaviour is so universal, the majority of economic subjects being so familiar with it, that as with any other traits acquired through socialization it seems self-evidently *normal*. Different behaviour is consequently deviant, abnormal. Peasants reacting to a rise in the price of rice by growing less of it, because the desired income is now assured with less effort, are deemed to be acting irrationally.

For anthropologists tradition
Remains the major inhibition
And peasants oftener than we think
When led to water, do not drink.

Apparently a totally different social impulse operates here, also learned, a cultural trait passed on in socialization and determining behaviour. This observation should really suffice: in these matters things are the way they are because that's the way they are. In social science we cannot resign ourselves to this state of affairs. Therefore this behaviour is reduced in theoretical speculation to the existence of 'constraints' this world-view puts on all things which a 'normal' human being would find desirable. In this conception there is no abundance of anything, there is only scarcity. If one person claims more for himself, another will receive less. Such a society in this theory's conception, is dominated by the idea of a 'limited good' (Foster, 1965). One is reminded of the antiquarian economic theory of mercantilism, to which there applied this kind of central concept of irreproduceability, while at the same time an 'organic community' was postulated - a most pleasing idea to contemporary protagonists of the 'limited good' concept in the Limits to Growth form. Although some may feel that this state of bliss is marred by the fact that the scarcity of resources and their distribution give rise to what in every introduction to economics is called the 'price commodity' - money. The valuation of everything in terms of money and prices is then explained as a concession to the nauseating middle classes smothering all Flower Power. Did Mao not say poignantly 'Let a thousand flowers blossom'?

THE RATIONAL ECONOMY

That economists face the danger of man becoming one-dimensional or alienated so undauntedly, is less attributable to their personal courage than to their unfamiliarity with the risks involved. They continue to aver that an increase in prices creates incentives. Thus Linneman is confident that world food production and distribution can be improved by a 'relatively high, stable international price level for food' (1975, 8). And industrialists in a poor country who ignore abundant supplies of cheap labour and opt for capital-intensive production - the very behaviour vilified as irrational by the casual observer - are really very much concerned with considerations of price. A whole range of factors has come into play which lower the price of capital. For a start, there is the protection against competition as a result of import restrictions. Where production is planned for the substitution of previously imported goods, the price can be fixed to cover even unnecessarily high costs. The same applies to production under license, because as the patent-holders accumulate royalties they have no desire to expose the product to competition by granting licenses to other parties. Further protection is provided by the overvalued local currency which artificially keeps down the price of imported capital goods. And if in addition investment is subsidized as part of a national development strategy, the price of the factor capital falls even more. 'Equipment', concludes Tinbergen, 'has become accessible at too low a price and for this reason businessmen are inclined to make incorrect decisions' (1973, 5).

Against this all kinds of influences combine to force up the price of the labour factor. The productivity of workers as yet unhabituated to factory work and insufficiently trained will probably be low, the more so since management cannot be most effective at this stage. Political life seems to flourish somewhat earlier than economic life: it is not unknown for an underdeveloped country to have a comprehensive network of social legislation including provisions for a minimum wage, redundancy payments, job security, and restrictions on shiftwork. These achievements, however, inflate the price of labour. Trade unions also press demands for improved conditions of employment. These influences lead to a situation where the industrialist in the modern sector of a developing country has more machines and less workers in his factory than would otherwise be the case. But these influences do not reach beyond the modern sector. Outside of it, where enterprises do not receive subsidies or protection, where labour legislation does not apply or is not complied with, where unionization has made no impact - there one would find a relationship between capital and labour that has been uncontaminated by price distortion.

Just now the term 'organic' cropped up: its complement will have to be evoked as well: 'natural balance'. When price distortion has thrown the economy off course, then correct prices should provide the incentives to get back on course and restore the balance of scarcity relationships. 'Get the relative factor prices right' (Cooper, 1972, 13). But if this implies the repeal of social legislation, the banning of trade unions and cuts in subsidies, then the proposal does not seem a viable one. It means also that governments in fact cannot pursue a development policy at all, and for the poor countries such a 'balance' would be tantamount to a return to nature.

When the economic planner is not happy with market prices, which reflect the disequilibria inherent in the very state of underdevelopment, he corrects these in the so-called shadow prices.

The local price of capital may be lower than the rate charged on the world market, because institutions such as the World Bank tend to offer soft terms, which would lead to the choice of a production process creating few work places. In the interest of employment, the shadow price for capital may then be established at a level where labour-intensive production becomes feasible. As all the industrial projects the plan calls for are subjected to similar arithmetics, a number emerge as viable propositions. Apart from these adjustments to world market conditions, shadow prices also reflect political objectives, to the extent that a lower rate of growth is condoned in the event that the spreading of income, achieved through the liberal application of labour, is given priority.

As against the option of allowing a majority of labour incomes to increase gradually over a longer period of time - but right from the start - the alternative strategy is to raise the wage level more precipitously - but after a period of constancy; the latter is associated with large-scale investment.

The individual entrepreneur, confronted with a price at which he can sell competitively, reasons equally in retrograde fashion when comparing that price with his computed costs. But there is a vital difference, in that he abandons the project when the comparison leaves no worthwhile margin. A tax (levied on capital) or a subsidy (granted on employment) in this strategy is designed to dissuade him from purchasing advanced machinery - which is made expensive for him - and instead to recruit labour - which is made cheap for him. As said before, the argument outlined here can be found in the literature of development economics, although there are considerable differences of opinion regarding the content of the shadow price concept (Sen, 1975, 97ff.). The extent to which the instrument is effective depends on the extent to which prices indeed determine investment decisions, so that on the basis of price adjustments these decisions can be influenced.

For one thing, the price of a factor of production does not mean the same thing to an industrialist as to a planner, if only because the time span with which the former calculates is shorter. As far as the industrialist is concerned, he must be assured of an adequate return on investment before his machines have to be written off. In addition, the expansion of employment will benefit local enterprise only indirectly via the rise in purchasing power; an industrial strategy of an individual firm cannot be geared to this. An experiment with labour-intensive technology will bring the firm a remote advantage, while the uncertainties of all experimental methods of production are only too obvious. When the industrialist buys machines abroad, he knows at least that they will work; it must remain an open question whether an alternative technology will work. Because inevitably more labour will have to be hired, internal organization will become more complex - people are more volatile than machines. A local technician who is not very experienced in the production process inspires little confidence; a process designed by him is only cheaper if it actually works as well as other techniques. If the technician has been trained abroad, he will probably be more inclined to apply a technique with which he is familiar. If the industrialist turns to a foreign technician, this will apply even more. Industrialists in India have been found to adopt existing imported technology, even if successful local equivalents were available, 'owing to lack of confidence in the indigenous know-how'. Technical know-how is seen, not without justification, as a Western speciality, and local know-how is suspect (Cooper, 1974, 57).

The same approach is occasionally adopted by governments; the disposition was discussed earlier in connection with road construction which, though signally suited for labour-intensive procedures, is often left to foreign contractors who bring in the latest earthmoving equipment. A viable bio-gas project, whereby energy was produced by the fermentation of cow-dung, was ignored for a long time by the Indian government. Bhatt calls it 'a sad commentary on the ... power elite'. Tractors were ordered in Eastern Europe on the advice of Russian experts, even though an indigenous vehicle of equal merit was available (Bhatt, 1975, 659). Followers of the centre-periphery model contend that political elites, when confronted with a choice between more or less capital-intensive production methods, will choose the former because that is more in line with their own interests (Cooper, 1975, 177). The progressive Brouwer and Miedema, in turn, believe that intermediate technology is popular because it presents no dangers to the 'ruling class' (1975, 71). The content of truth seems dependent on the observer's standpoint. In neither of the two instances is this behaviour apparently based on a careful analysis of prices, costs and returns for industry and the economy as a whole.

Throughout the decades of development the primary goal has been to increase real incomes. In order to achieve this, the flow of goods of the agricultural and industrial sectors must be increased. As late as 1965 the eminent Kaldor wrote that'by increasing capital per worker tenfold, you increase output per worker twentyfold' (Stewart, 1977, 106). Consequently he urged developing countries to avail themselves of the latest technology.

The priority of employment creation is in conflict with the above. Moreover, the utilization of any technique but the most advanced will cause an economy to fall behind in the path of development which, in the view of Kaldor and other development economists, all economies are expected to follow. No government will choose to be among the also-rans. Zero-growth and conservation of natural resources are not among the priorities of Third World countries.

A review of the events since the need for development of the Third World has been recognized evinces so many impulses to the transfer of large-scale technology that it is not surprising that only the actual failure of this experiment has forced the realization that a grave error was committed.

Here is the historical parallel: our understanding of the nature of wealth is dictated by our experience of industrialization. The demonstration effect has brought forth an identical perception of wealth and prosperity among the populations of non-industrialized countries. Prosperity for large sections of them requires mass production and standardization, which are provided only by machines. All kinds of consumer goods and means of production can be manufactured on a large scale only. The obvious and hence long-defended model of import substitution leads to a modern industrial mode of production: the manufacture on the home market of factory products which were previously imported means the duplication of foreign production processes if the consumer is to be offered a product of similar quality and price.

The opposite strategy of export-orientation requires the processing of raw materials and primary products into a form which will fetch a good price on the world market.

The demands of quality and consistency are fulfilled by organizing production on the model of that of the industrial countries - again large scale.

Differences in exchange rates aimed at checking imports and boosting exports leave the strategy with loopholes which local businessmen are quick to exploit. Then there is the point that the accumulation of capital, which makes further expansion possible, is best served by broadly conceived projects. Multinational corporations, finally, show a tendency to transplant to developing countries almost unaltered production processes which have proven successful at home. Adaptation occurs incidentally; the trusted large-scale process is the starting point.

6 Impediments to omniscience

'The beauty of Economic Man was that one knew exactly what he was after.' (Whitehead)

Comte may have proclaimed sociology the queen of the sciences, students of this and related disciplines have on the whole in all humility refrained from judging - let alone condemning - the behaviour they were studying in their fellow men.

Not that they had no pride, or did not think there were alternatives, or that the alternatives designed by them would not lead to a better society. The social utopias show that in the past the study of society has inspired attempts at evolving more acceptable social formations.

Economics above all continued to be practised according to the rigid rules of natural science: the object of study was treated as an objective datum and personal likes and dislikes were of no import. At least not on a conscious level. But the fact that social forces were discussed as if they were natural forces, which pushed economic theory in the direction of a kind of social mechanics, shows that personal approach and subjective preferences did permeate the premises of the subject.

For the view that social behaviour ought to be studied as if it is a natural phenomenon also expresses a preference colouring the outcome of scientific activity.

When it was realized that objective investigation of an area in which the researcher himself is a participant is inherently impossible, precisely because of the coincidence of subject and object, theorists turned to the conscious application of criteria.

An obvious choice is the application of the test of efficiency to the organization of economic life. For this the economist need not venture far from home: he confines himself to the sphere of prices and wages. But why should one restrict oneself to this yardstick? A society should surely not be judged by the norms that govern the performance of a business enterprise. What matters is the wellbeing of people, and other criteria will apply here. In the 1930s a welfare theory was formulated which contemporary advocates of both growth and zero-growth may find acceptable.

GOOD AND EVIL

The same phenomena - industrial growth, economic development - are assessed differently at different times. The professional judges who call themselves social scientists are not exempt from this rule. Although the scientific ideal of objectivity, which endeavours to separate knowledge ('is') from judgment ('ought'), has been relinquished by them, the individual value judgments which are now happily used in its stead are sometimes asserted so strongly that they take the form of a new objectivity. Drobyshev and Vafa, for instance, warn that 'Problems of technology are increasingly becoming problems which disturb writers, artists and composers' (1974, 211). Whoever would like to adapt technology so that artists are no longer disturbed by it is free to put forward proposals, but he should not be surprised if he fails to elicit response from a majority. One has the impression that the social scientists of a radical mould set their sights higher: the lack of response seems to confirm to them that the alienated masses do not know what is good for them. For Galtung et al., good is synonymous with 'Personal growth' (1975, 523). For the signatories of the Lund Letter it is 'qualitative rather than quantitative growth' (1977, 8). But not all that long ago most observers, including those trained in the social sciences, valued economic growth highly. To go by their political-economic utterances, those burdened with administrative responsibilities still stress the importance of growth. Where growth has stalled, governments have done all in their power to restart it. While the ideologues, paraphrasing Blake, vary the theme of 'dark, satanic mills', trade unionists seem to adhere to the adage that smoking chimneys mean wealth.

Here, two views are expressed which have appeared alternately in the history of the West. At the level of the ecopathology of everyday life one hears, besides appreciative noises on the subject of progress ('Distances don't count these days'), discomfort with change ('There's nothing to be done about it), fear of decline ('Trees don't grow to heaven') and unconcern ('I won't live to see the day'). At the level of thought this is paralleled by the optimistic ontological vision of the Kingdom of Heaven or the workers' paradise as the outcome of the imminent movement towards the good. In reference to Prometheus, knowledge is power, and knowing men are expected to subjugate nature, to become 'maîtres et possesseurs de la nature' (Descartes). In economics, this confidence in man's own ability is expressed in the proclamation that 'since Keynes' we possess the means to control developments, or at least 'correct' unwanted developments. The texts which announced the so-called development decades of the United Nations at times seem to say 'name your growth rate and we will tell you how to achieve it'. The West Indian development economist Lewis told the sceptics why they should rejoice. More goods after all mean more real wealth, he reminded us. And if that is not persuasive enough, consider also that there will be greater freedom of choice - a spiritual benefit which, according to Lewis, answers to the most profound human wishes.

But doubts could not be dispelled altogether. The equation of more with better is lately brought to bear only in the sphere of development aid, as Bauer remarks (1976, 22). German observers, traditionally strong in critique of civilization, coined the term 'consumption athletics' for the surfeit of available goods - an open fireplace, two cars, subscriptions to 'Vogue' and 'Country Life' - and still the full life is not achieved. Lewis's complacent notion of freedom of choice was upset by Galbraith, who showed that the sovereignty of the consumer is a theoretical fiction. The loss of a job due to automation infringes a worker's right to work and challenges his human dignity. The worker who does have a job loses his identity in the drudgery of work, becomes alienated. His dignity is not upheld either - according to Galtung et al. he becomes 'incapable of deeper love' (1975, 525). Where there was still some economic growth Mishan showed its 'costs' to be prohibitive. The hubris of the moment now fosters in Western society and in value-oriented science a mood of rejection of *all* development. 'You can't win!', as the Americans say. Our technical capacity, once a source of pride, is denigrated mercilessly. Decentralists, distributists, populists, anarchists and minarchists reject all industrialism, be it capitalist or socialist. 'Industrialization is a disease!' (Allahwerdi, 1974, 67).

People meditate following Schumacher, the well-known Buddhist convert, or hibernate following Thoreau, the prophet of self-sufficiency. Both are seen as the forerunners of the new cosmic consciousness. Modern technology appears as evil: exhaustion of natural resources, disasters caused by man's tampering with nature and the nuclear holocaust are the first associations it evokes. The big cities, conurbations made possible by technology, are no longer appreciated as centres of art and science, as foci of creativity where progress is forged, but vilified as hotbeds of crime. The big aeroplanes, formerly admired for their speed, are now - even though they fly even faster - restricted in their landing rights. There is growing disenchantment with speed, mass and noise. The desire for the small, the tranquil and the rural is redolent of the past, when everything was more relaxed, more tranquil and, what is more, cheaper. Then the division of labour was not as far advanced and, in accordance with Marx's ideal of labour, man could fish in the morning, hunt in the afternoon and philosophize, perhaps censure society, in the evening, instead of being occupied with the same thing all day, so that some people never get a chance of going hunting or fishing because by virtue of their profession they have to censure society all day. How delightful it must have been to travel no faster than a horse's gallop. Huxley was right: 'The industrial revolution brought the vice of speed.' Illich correlates speed to social justice, which in his view declines as speed increases (1973, 116). The image of the innocent noble savage, satisfied with the little he has and living in harmony with nature and with his fellows, attains concrete shape in Sahlin's 'Stone Age economics'. In a chapter on 'the original affluent society' he sifts through the anthropological literature in search of indications of prosperity despite scarcity of resources. Scarcity, as Polanyi surmised, occurs only where markets develop. The Australian aborigines knew no markets, 'and I can only say that I have always found the greatest abundance in their huts' (quoted from Grey in 1841). The same applied to the Bushmen: 'they lived in a kind of material plenty' (Sahlin, 1972, 9).

DREAM AND REALITY

One wonders to what extent these verdicts are based on objective observation, especially considering the fact that in the instance of the tribe mentioned by Grey, contemporary commentators speak of famines, while the same writer reported that this abundance does not include food and water.... In a contribution to a conference of the Past and Present Society, Ranger suggests that many of the traditions ascribed to pre-colonial Africa have been 'invented' by Europeans. The British colonial administrator, himself often imbued with a reverence for tradition, wanted above all to select from the tribal culture that which he saw as good. So he saw stability and social immutability, and tried to respect it. 'African society was seen as profoundly conservative, living within age-old rules which did not change ... an ideology based on the absence of change ... a clearly defined hierarchical status ... it was intended as a compliment to the admirable qualities of tradition' (Ranger, 1977, 73ff.). In settling disputes, British colonial jurisdiction took account of what were thought to be local customs. These became inviolable as they were recorded or even codified, although, Ranger believes, in many cases they were no more than the fabrications of British administrators. The claims of African parties were weighed against the stipulations of this supposed customary law. 'Those whose traditions lost a case came back a year or two later with better traditions' (Ranger, 1977, 76). Binsbergen, quoted by Ranger, goes even further when he calls the Central African tribes a creation of the European authorities and African intellectuals. Stokes contends that a similar idealization of conditions occurred in India. Well-intentioned British administrators concocted an image of the 'co-sharing, egalitarian and self-governing Indian village community as the immemorial bedrock of Indian society, an image which gave the lie to the notion that the British found India in a condition of destructive anarchy in which the only property of the soil belonged to the despotic rulers'. Wilkes, Elphinstone, Metcalfe and others are dismissed by Stokes as the designers of 'idyllic accounts'. These were taken up by Indian nationalists and disseminated as the Golden Age before the arrival of the British. Stokes sees Gandhi's ideal of the self-sufficient and self-governing Indian village community as the outcome of this, originally British, vision, and he points out that even the name of the village socialism movement, Sarvodaya, derives from Ruskin's 'Unto His Last' (1978, 121).

In our post-colonial days the period of European imperialism is regarded as pernicious, and the deplorable political or economic conditions obtaining in the former colonies are presented as the consequence of colonial interference with the culture in question. It is alleged that the affluence of the pre-colonial societies described by Sahlin came to an end with imperialist exploitation. The occasional defender of colonialism may note that some former colonies have become prosperous while others, including tropical countries which have never been colonized, are languishing economically (Bauer, 1976, 148). But this is not the point. What matters is that the spirit of the age, which is anti-colonialist, prefers to take refuge in the almost paradisiac legends of tropical areas still uncontaminated by imperialism, rather than acknowledge the equally evident reports of abject poverty, disease and exploitation by an indigenous ruling group. In trying to assess a wide-ranging development strategy which abandons certain technologies and experimentally replaces them with others, one will find it useful to trace the origin of some ideas and to assess their impact during certain periods, so that their relative importance can be borne in mind.

The history of Europe offers slightly more factual material, although this too is described selectively, and the past sometimes appears in a romantic light. Admittedly Polanyi provides no detailed assessment of the old, patriarchal society, but he does seem to interpret it positively. As Kindleberger has remarked, the same attitude is found in the writers on industrial development in England: 'the Hammonds, Martineau, Marx and Engels ... painted the miseries of the lives of the poor under the factory system, thereby implying that the status quo ante was a happy one' (1973, 47). Hayek shows that those who gave evidence to the royal commissions which prepared the New Poor Law of 1834 were primarily aggrieved landowners, who had little cause to look favourably on industrialization. Be that as it may, the statistician King divided the population of England in 1688 into two groups: 2,675,000 who augmented the wealth of the nation and 2,825,000 who reduced it. The latter category defines the poor, subdivided into 1,375,000 workers and servants, 1,300,000 paupers, 66,000 small freeholders, the remainder being simply designated 'tramps'. 'There were poor and poor laws well before the commercial revolution and the industrial revolution and when there were crop failures, suffering was widespread' (Kindleberger, 1973, 48). It is also known and demonstrable that the average life expectancy rose gradually, as did the average height, which is indicative of an improved diet.

In the reflections on the ideal form of economic life one can sense a yearning for the past, a past of rural peacefulness, when the organic prevailed over the inorganic and the food cycle was closed. In this kind of society, provided it could be recreated, human values would, according to Harper, once again come first. These are 'best served indirectly ... in consumption rather than in production' (1973, 289). But to make consumption possible, there must be production, no matter on how limited a scale. Those who subscribe to the alienation syndrome oppose the disjunction of the two activities brought about in industrial organization. In the self-sufficient rural economy they are fully integrated, and it is therefore consistent that some who reject industrial society envisage a commune based on agricultural production. Thoreau's 'Walden' and his Dutch counterpart Van Eeden's 'Walden' appeal to the imagination. Following their example, like-minded groups begin to cultivate the land; they, if we are to believe the claims of the small-is-beautiful-crowd, form the vanguard of a new, decentralized economic life. Arrêteau, anthropologist and radical social critic (the spirit of contradiction has been in his family since the Huguenots, as he himself reports), has described his experiences with an experiment of this kind in France. To begin with, he impresses upon his reader that he takes his choice seriously: 'The style of living technocrats would impose on me I don't want at any price' (1973, 311). Of the other members of the commune he expects a certain perseverance, even when nature throws up obstacles. Nevertheless he respects the argument that the flesh is weak: 'They are not accustomed to being compelled to work regularly.' Of the approximately 500 people who had been members of the group since its foundation, only four had had previous experience of farm labour. The tasks allocated to each individual were rarely completed. 'Working several hours consecutively on the same job struck them as repugnant. Indeed, no one had the least idea what it means to work all day.' But there were lengthy debates on how to structure and organize the work: 'We lost an incredible amount of time speechifying.' Arrêteau remarks that while the members happily embraced the concept of farming life, they found everyday farmwork repugnant. He observes that they did not crave possessions, with the notable exception of a car. 'Almost all have cars - the last thing they want to let go, precisely so as to avoid becoming isolated.' Contact with the despised industrial world is maintained. Only two of every hundred completed the apprenticeship. It was above all the hard work with simple tools that most found daunting. Arrêteau is not surprised: 'Traditional technology requires a lot of hard work, which is exactly why people gave it up.

The rejection of technology had gained currency even when by present standards technology was still crude. Spengler in 'Decline of the West', Huxley in 'Brave New World', Fromm in 'Fear of Freedom', portrayed technology in the 1930s as an evil, and Orwell predicted in 1948 that it would be far worse in 1984 - so from now only a few years to go until the abyss.

In the meantime people have become alarmed. In industrial society, industry is now widely considered a source of misery, a destroyer of nature and humanity. 'Society is being destroyed by the growth of non-convivial tools' (Agosin, 1976, 15). But salvation is possible by switching to tools which are 'convivial'. 'The crisis can be solved if we learn to invert the present deep structure of tools' (Illich, 1974, 340). Illich's 'tools for conviviality' will remove the evil aspects of modern society. Technology must be simplified, wrested from the capitalist, and brought back to human proportions. We will then learn again how to be thrifty - Heilbroner's 'parsimonious attitudes' - while rediscovering the pleasure of life - Boulding's 'joying' (1976, 72).

The thought suggests itself that the economically underdeveloped nations are in this respect better off, that in fact we have nothing to teach them at all. On the contrary, we can learn from them.

Take the Thais: 'The Thai view of life is something to be enjoyed here and now.' This is precisely what Western parents try to keep their children - for whom they want the best - away from, so that by deferred gratification they can 'make good' later in life. Yet the Thais 'work rather for happiness than for material gain' (Ayal, 1963, 46). Schumacher was greatly impressed with the Buddhist economy, which knows no urbanization, no industry and hardly any import and export (1977). He extols the carefreeness, the simplicity and the non-violence he found in Burma. The absence of labour-saving machinery and consumer goods, which was once seen as evidence of the poverty that an effective development strategy was to alleviate, now becomes the hallmark of the good life. Thus the fulfilment of limited consumer wishes, those that are 'proper', takes over as the objective of development strategy from the raising of consumption to Western levels. In the old value-free days of economics, 'need' was accepted as a given. The economist made no judgment as to the desirability or reprehensibility of its fulfilment. The choice of technology was limited to alternatives which led to the product for which demand existed. As Boon, whose work on factor relationships has been referred to earlier, says unequivocally: 'The product, although made by alternative methods, must be of equal quality' (1964, 12). This puts practical limits on the range of production possibilities. For even if there are differences in factor costs, it is still conceivable that relatively capital-intensive methods will be preferred for the simple reason that some goods cannot be produced in any other way.

LUXURY AND WANT

Economists declined to make judgments on needs not so much out of a sense of humility but because they were committed to a model that presupposed competition and saw the judgment of the consumer as the outcome of a process of income-formation and spending which is integral to economic life as described in the model. The scheme left room for changes of preference. As incomes rose, the consumption of particular goods was reduced in favour of others which, by virtue of their being related to a higher standard of living, were considered more luxurious. This phenomenon was described in the nineteenth century by Engels, whose remarks suggest that the part of income spent on food falls relatively as income rises. Another cause of changing needs lies in the production techniques themselves, which, as they become more advanced, produce improved or even totally new goods satisfying the same category of needs. This too has been known for a long time. It was Say who wrote that 'repousser une machine nouvelle c'est repousser un produit nouveau' (Heertje, 1973, 28). Yet not all incomes rise evenly and technological advances do not benefit all consumers equally. Some cross the line between what was first thought 'luxury' to what is now deemed 'necessary' earlier than others. Considerations of equality and justice then prompt the attempts to determine a certain norm below which no groups should be allowed to fall. When all incomes rise gradually, an ever larger part of luxury consumption passes into the sphere of 'minimum necessity'. Rowntreee has carried out three famous studies on the 'poverty' line in Britain. The real income of the minimum he decided on in 1936 lay 48 per cent above the level worked out in 1899, and when he repeated his observations in 1950 he arrived at a norm which was another 18 per cent higher. Similar experiences are reported from France and the United States, where attempts have also been made to establish such norms (Fiegehen et al., 1977; Marceau, 1977). Because we are dealing with market economies, the norm is always expressed in money incomes. At a different point in time within the same economy, the norm becomes insignificant; for the same or a different point in time outside that economy it becomes meaningless. The norms which are applied in America to determine the amount of relief made available to the poor exceed the standard of living of the majority of the world's population (Scitovsky, 1976, 108). Such minimum norms have been worked out in developing countries, but these are more like target figures than minimum subsistence levels.

Thus Nairobi City Council established a norm for town dwellings; construction costs amount to £1000 - which the citizens are quite unable to afford.

One can in fact live under a wide variety of housing conditions: in a penthouse where the air-conditioning compensates for the overwarm and cosy log fire (Park Avenue, New York); in a packing case which has been put on its side so that the lid serves as a door (Dakar); it is even possible to limit one's shelter for the night to a few tiles on the pavement (Calcutta). To avoid the pitfalls of comparison, efforts are now concentrated on establishing minimum norms for a number of categories of need, taking into account point of time, climate, income, locally available materials, and so on. The recent realization of the limits set to world development has also altered the evaluation of these norms. Again they present little more than a target figure - a level towards which a strategy of development, if successful, will lead the majority of the world's population.

Social thought is subject to the changes in the social and economic climate. To put it bluntly: the social scientist sets his sails to every wind. If society is experiencing a period of prosperity, he views the conduct of his fellow men with optimism. He sees himself as offering guidance, so that the harmonious outcome may be partly attributable to this expert navigation. Economists have looked upon the post-war period of growth in Europe and America with some satisfaction: it was the science of economics that had made it all possible. When the downturn loomed, the intellectual climate also changed. The social upheaval that subsequently occurred admittedly could not have been foreseen, but it was explained afterwards: the harmony model had failed. Conflict was a central feature of an industrial society whose constituent social groups had opposing interests.

This society now was seen as inherently evil; the decline in its (growth) potential was not really surprising. According to the new social theory, the obsessional pursuit of a single objective - growth for the sake of growth - had avenged itself. This society did not only appear inhuman, it was inhumane.

7 Basic needs of the needy

> 'The quantitative is of preponderant weight only at the lowest level of Being' (Schumacher)

Human beings have needs and economics studies how they satisfy them. Initially the science was pursued, as shown earlier, without pre-judgment, or at most with a prejudice that was not acknowledged at the level of conscious thought. Scientific objectivity thus meant that the needs, which manifested themselves as market demands for certain goods in the economic system, were accepted as given. It was not denied that the level of gratification was for some groups lower than for others, but this conception of economics did not permit the deduction that there were corresponding subjective differences in wealth. Perhaps the man with less money to spend had fewer needs - who was to know? He could still feel reasonably prosperous. No doubt he also found satisfaction from other sources, sources not valued in money terms; for this aspect the quaint term 'psychic income' was coined.

Once serious economists had taken up the normative position, and a person with a high income was frankly believed to be more prosperous than the average wage earner, the step to the ideology of equality was bound to follow. The day when the minimum wage became the target of economic policy was near.

SHEER SUBSISTENCE

The classical economic concept of 'need' was thus given a new content, or rather, a new accent on the received content. Further study of consumer behaviour had already supplied an insight into the complexity of needs. It became clear that apart from an obvious utility function, the desired goods had to have additional characteristics.

The consumer does not judge a product solely on its use-value. He buys clothes not only to protect himself against rain and cold, but also because he is a follower of fashion, because he likes certain colours, because he wants to conform to a group norm or go against it. When only a small number of consumers can afford a certain product, its possession confers distinction upon them: this was once the case with the two- or four-horse carriage, it is now the case with the six- or eight-cylinder car. In the 1950s much was written about the symbolic function of certain goods; it seemed that increasing wealth would always coincide with extension and improvement of the range of consumer goods. Since then an apparent return to utility has taken place in some quarters: coarser materials and less elaborate cuts are preferred, the 'military look' of transistor radios is popular, furniture should be simple and all kinds of adornments are frowned upon. These preferences do not signify a decline in wealth, far from it. They are indicative of a shift in the social meaning of consuming in a society overwhelmed with goods produced by a highly advanced industrial apparatus. Here the previously perhaps slightly less manifest correlation between 'value' in the economic sense and 'value' in the social sense is revealed. Kluckhohn's definition of value as a 'conception of the desirable' covers both: 'Man (is) a creature who entertains concepts, turns them into goals and seeks to realize those goals in action' (Shriver, 1972, 532). Social change then becomes tantamount to a shift in goals, and in economic action this leads to a shift in the evaluation of certain means of gratification. In this model, causality runs from 'value' in the social sphere to 'value' in the economic sphere. Prosperity - a condition in which needs are satisfied - is never reached, because the value system, influenced partly by the level of satisfaction reached, undergoes constant changes. Thus the causal link also operates in reverse: what is found worth striving for in the present is in part determined by what the past striving for wealth has yielded. It now becomes possible for the satisfaction of *economic* needs to be placed lower down in the hierarchy of values. Something on these lines is advocated by Schumacher, who wishes to draw a distinction between worldly goods, whose benefits are 'ephemeral', and eternal goods. 'True development' then means: less need for economic goods and more need for religious or philosophical development (Schumacher, 1975, 20). It is not necessary to accept Schumacher's religious preference: in the conception of industrial man as being enslaved to the machine, a reduction of the needs fulfilled by industry signifies an advance in itself. The French school of Perroux, similarly, would like to replace the term 'développement' by 'libération'.

Other writers, avoiding entering into the treacherous realm of an exact definition of 'basic human needs', speak neither of religious transcendence nor of liberation from social chains, but suggest that man is (or at least ought to be) striving towards self-realization. But without a precise definition of this 'self', the term is much too vague, and certainly an insufficient basis on which to build a development policy. Maslow has devised a series of categories of need which, with successive satisfaction, lead to higher stages - although again it is not quite clear to higher stages of what. Physical needs should be satisfied first: food, water, sleep, shelter. These are followed by the need for security, for 'belongingness'.

The 'basic needs' notion which has been under discussion in recent years in fact presupposes such a hierarchy: a development strategy must be directed in the first place to the satisfaction of basic needs (here arising out of physiology).

It is worth maintaining a degree of analytic clarity at this juncture, the more so because we are no longer engaged in open-ended speculation, but are dealing with considerations on the basis of which - if the politicians in power in the developing countries accept them - a very specific policy would be implemented that would affect the way of life of a great number of people. It is, as the econometrician Cannegieter remarks, not too difficult to establish what satisfies a cat, for one need only listen to her purring; but for someone from one society to determine for someone else, living in another society, what is good for him not only goes much further, it is also considerably less reliable (1974, 13). In this respect economists have come far since the days when they did not even dare pronounce on the desirability or undesirability of income differentials, on the grounds that one could never know how wage earners experienced their position internally. 'Interpersonal comparison', denounced then, is applied freely now: development economists prescribe to a consumer living in a poor country which of his needs are 'basic' and which are not; at the same time they tell him that it is for his own good and for the good of all mankind to strive only for the satisfaction of this particular category of needs. So, for instance, Rattner deems the water-closet, invented by Alexander Cumming in 1779, not basic for developing countries: 'An example of an inadequate product' (1975, 303). Stewart takes exception to some improvements made in the construction industry of these countries, which have led to an unnecessary improvement of quality. '(This is) the opposite of what might be thought of as appropriate product innovation' (1977, 42).

Such views depend wholly on a particular choice of norms. For the Club of Rome the chance of survival in the long term was what mattered, and since this is also served by the restriction of an undeniably basic need like eating, the Club proposed 'to reduce the rate of food production by 20%' (Forrester, 1972, 14ff.). Speaking of the quality of life as a whole creates an impression of objectivity, particularly if the concept of quality is not explained further. Whose 'life' is at issue is not explained either. In the industrial countries the flow of goods has been so steady and large for years that - as predicted by the marginality principle of economic theory - the quantities fail to fascinate anyone any more. The category of quality is transformed, higher things come to mind - such as justice and self-realization. Schumacher saw the Burmese solution, in which everyone is his own monk, as a shining example. Next to the idea that only on the basis of a certain degree of wealth do 'higher' goals become attainable, and its opposite - also frequently heard - that only abstinence will lead to the attainment of 'higher' goals, the concept of 'basic needs' appears as a strange compromise. Its tenet is that the best base is the small base - limited wealth. To those who decry technology as a source of ruin, such half-heartedness must be abhorrent. But more important are the thoughts of those directly affected, the inhabitants of the poor countries. At a conference of church leaders in Geneva, Ellul, author of the gloomy volume 'La Technique', inveighed against the evils of industrial society. Many more speeches echoed much the same sentiment. But a young African countered that his country first wanted a chance to experience the problems described. Technology meant for the majority of Africans that life would become easier: 'It means that our women will no longer have to walk five miles to the river for water every day; and it means that when it gets dark, instead of going to sleep we can stay up and read a book' (Shriver, 1972, 550f.).

BEYOND SUBSISTENCE

McCall approves of the definition of the quality of life offered by the Environmental Protection Agency: 'By quality of life we mean an individual's satisfaction of his needs over a period of time' (1975, 236). This approach assumes that indicators of levels of gratification can be found. Besides taking into account wage levels, hours of work and pension plans, 'job satisfaction' includes an evaluation of *satisfaction* with wages, working hours, and so on. A survey in the United States showed that 85 per cent of those asked reported themselves at least 'somewhat' satisfied and only 15 per cent 'dissatisfied' (McCall, 1975, 23). In recent years the view has gained currency that satisfaction with income is determined above all by its relative level. Even if income is adequate to provide for the satisfaction of 'basic needs', a person may still be dissatisfied because many others have an income which enables them to satisfy all kinds of needs which are anything but 'basic'.

The spectators who are the first to arrive to see the Queen are assured a good view by standing on their toes to look over the line of police officers. But as the crowd gathers this behaviour becomes a source of aggravation. Above average height is then a gift of nature which gives some a better view - just as the mentally and physically well endowed have an advantage over the rest despite all the equality of opportunity in the distribution of income. Spectators who are not tall enough and do not get to see the Queen may take comfort in the realization that height can be a disadvantage in other respects - for instance in the selection of marriage partners.

In the sphere of incomes there is a similar consolation: 'money isn't everything'. A study on 'rank happiness' in the United States confirmed that in the period from 1946 to 1970, when real incomes per head rose by 62 per cent, the ratio of groups considering themselves 'very happy', 'fairly happy' and 'not too happy' remained almost unchanged. But among those whose incomes had risen faster than the average, the level of happiness had also risen. Another study found that the number of happy people in every higher income bracket was almost unchangeably greater than in the lower brackets. Happy were only 20 per cent of those earning less than $ 1000; in the $ 5000 to $ 6000 bracket the figure was 37 per cent; above $ 15000 53 per cent. Unhappy were 23 per cent of those earning less than $ 1000, against only 8 per cent in the over $ 15000 bracket (Scitovsky, 1976, 134-7). As an interfering factor, it should be taken into consideration that work satisfaction among higher-income earners is likely to be greater.

Several studies in different European countries have shown that during the years of economic boom, when real incomes of the different social groups rose steadily, the satisfaction derived from the yearly wage rise outweighed the dissatisfaction with the inequality of income distribution. But when the economy stagnated, the idea suggested itself that in a redistribution the lower income brackets should benefit. There has been an animated debate in the industrial countries on the distribution of income. Against this background it is not surprising that the inequality of world incomes, and the skewed distribution of incomes within the poor countries, have also attracted greater attention.

Once human needs have outgrown the status of givens and have been classified in categories, the temptation arises to rank them. Greater value could be attached, for instance, to spiritual needs. And the satisfaction of economic needs could, from a particular point onwards, be thought to put constraints on the realization of primary spiritual values.

On the other hand, it is said that the consumer at the base of this pyramid of need, provided he is not removed from the world in religious transcendence, still considers a degree of material satisfaction to be of primary importance. As an Indonesian economist once told me: 'You only start to think about self-realization and alienation when you've had enough of rice and curry'.

8 Income distribution and redistribution

> 'Just as the fingers of the hand are of different length, so are some men older, healthier, richer, wiser than others.' (Yoruba saying)

Because in recent years the term stagnation has been bandied about so much, it is worth pointing out that national incomes have been calculated with any degree of accuracy only since the Second World War, and even then in only a few countries. Diachronic comparisons within the national economy, from which the growth rate is calculated, have only been possible for a limited number of years, and comparisons of national growth rates between countries are not very reliable. Most of the indices on which world figures are based are comparable to determining one's position by dead reckoning, a picture reminiscent of raising a wet finger to determine the wind direction. Every insider knows this. If the figures do not tally with his (political) conviction he can all too easily cast doubt upon the accuracy of the statistical material. Thus, it is possible to maintain that, even though the figures of distribution of income in a number of European countries point to a growing equality, labour is still being exploited.

LA BELLE EPOQUE

Growth and distribution of income are evidently matters where knowledge is coloured by the preferences of the scientist. In the 1970s the falling growth rate in the industrial economies prompted serious worries about the survival of Western civilization, even though it would be more accurate to regard the period 1948-73 as historically exceptionally favourable - a period which Kahn has dubbed 'La Deuxième Belle Epoque' (the first being between 1886 and 1913). The slow growth of the Third World economies compared to the target figures set by the United Nations in the two development decades and the dawning post-colonial awareness of widespread poverty, have given rise to pessimism regarding the results achieved. Yet the growth rate of a number of poor countries differs only marginally from that reached by rich countries in their initial period of development. Much has been written on this. According to a recent publication, 'The Measure of Poverty', more than 800 books and articles have appeared on the situation in America alone. But this is not germane to the discussion here. Let it suffice to note that the average growth of real GDP per head for the period 1950-70 was 2.2 per cent in Latin America; 4.8 per cent in the Middle East; 2.8 per cent in the Far East; 1.6 per cent in South Asia; and 2.1 per cent in Africa (Lipton, 1977, 426). There is sufficient reason to assume that this does not compare unfavourably with the first Belle Epoque of the rich countries. Although it is difficult to persuade some people to accept it, there are clear indications that the less privileged classes have gradually received a larger portion of what economists invariably call 'the cake' (Pen, 1974 and 1977). The explanation for this should be sought less in the magnanimity of the suppliers of capital and more in the greater relative scarcity of labour and in the efforts of trade unions. The phenomenon is known as the 'trickling-down effect': gradually, and increasingly, wealth will reach the lower income brackets.

However, it is far from certain whether the working class in Europe has been able to share in the fruits of progress from the beginning. On this again the figures supplied by various sources fail to provide conclusive evidence. The view that economic development has brought greater *in*equality is particularly persistent (this is consistent with the view that the pre-industrial era was more paradisal and hence more equal). As a general historical pattern this probably cannot be proven; in fact, in specific cases where figures are available, the opposite contention seems to be borne out. Thus Hill found that in the part of Africa she had studied there had been a pronounced inequality of incomes in the pre-colonial era (1977). Be that as it may, it is now undeniable that the 'trickling-down effect' has not or hardly at all been evident during the economic growth of the poor countries.

Figures on income distribution are even more difficult to come by than figures on aggregate income. As distribution changes, the constitution of the national product will also change, because the greater purchasing power of the lower income brackets will direct itself to different goods. The problems this creates may be illustrated by a simple example. Let us assume an economic production and consumption unit in which whisky is the sole luxury good and milk the sole staple. In a particular year, in which market forces determine prices and distribution, the national product consisted of 2 litres of whisky and 5 litres of milk. After correction of this injustice the national product consists of 1 litre of whisky and 10 litres of milk. But national income is not calculated in terms of commodities but in terms of prices, and these are partly determined by the general distribution of income. In the year of inequality, when the whisky-drinking elite oppressed the milk-drinking masses, whisky cost 20 monetary units (Mu) per litre and milk 2 Mu per litre. The national income was then

$$(2 \times 20) + (5 \times 2) = 50$$

After the redistribution it is

$$(1 \times 20) + (10 \times 2) = 40$$

In other words, the correction resulted in a fall of income. But if the market forces are allowed free reign, this will in turn be corrected because after the redistribution, the elite appears on the whisky market with less purchasing power and the majority will appear on the milk market with greater purchasing power. The outcome of both changes will force down the price of whisky and force up the price of milk. If, for instance, the price of whisky is halved and the price of milk doubled, the national income will be

$$(1 \times 10) + (10 \times 4) = 50$$

- that is - the same as in the first year. (Stewart and Streeten, 1971)

L'EPOQUE DES CRISES

Chenery, who has studied in detail the issues of growth and distribution, arrives at the following general estimate for the developing countries: the richest 20 per cent of the population claim 53 per cent of the national income; 40 per cent, the middle classes, claim 35 per cent; and 12 per cent are left for the poorest 40 per cent (1974). He concludes that, considering the low average income, the latter group suffers severe poverty. Lipton partly evades the problems of calculation and comparison by invoking Engels's law, which states that the proportion of income spent on food diminishes as incomes rise. In this case low-income groups will spend the greater proportion of their increased income on food, for the simple reason that they are underfed. This means that the rises in income which have occurred in the developing countries, in so far as they have accrued to the poor sections, should have resulted in a concomitant rise in food consumption (1977, 31).

The responsiveness of demand for goods to rises in income, that is, the extent to which a rise in income reflects on demand, is expressed as income elasticity of demand. For the population as a whole the proportion for the demand for food will be less than 1, since higher-income brackets expand their demand for food little or not at all. In this way, an average rise in income of 10 per cent will put up the demand for food in Southern Asia (excluding Japan) by 6.2 per cent, in Africa by 4 per cent and in Latin America by 3 per cent. Now if the average rise in income had been spread evenly, then in India, where income rose by 14 per cent between 1949/50 and 1968/69, a rise in food consumption by 32 per cent should have occurred. In fact the figure was 14 per cent. Price fluctuations cannot have influenced it, because food prices rose at about the same rate as prices generally. Perhaps the proportionate increase of young children, due to the decline of the infant mortality rate, depressed the required food intake per head, but the effects of these demographic changes are probably negligible. Similar calculations have been made for the Philippines, where between 1953 and 1969 income per head rose by 45 per cent, while food consumption per head merely rose by 15 per cent. In Mexico income per head rose by 41 per cent between 1953 and 1965, food consumption per head by 15 per cent.

On the basis of an - in itself not unsatisfactory - average rise in income per head for all developing countries of 75 per cent between 1950 and 1970, and assuming income elasticity and an equal distribution of the rise in income, a rise in caloric food intake per head of around 40 per cent was to be expected. The actual increase was less than 20 per cent.

Another approach to the distribution of income is found in the division between urban and rural. For a long time development economists accepted that it was pointless to distribute available funds equally over all sectors, since compensating forces would nullify any small improvements in wealth. It was thought better to create growth poles, the effects of which on income would be noticeable in other sectors of economic life, while as a focus of investment they would also have a better chance of success. Candidates for such concentrated effort were in the first instance industrial projects in the cities. Employment would be created, and the resultant greater purchasing power would in turn direct itself to the consumption of agricultural products, so that the rural areas would share, if only in the second instance, in the fruits of what was initially an industrial investment. Writers on distribution of income are mostly of the opinion that this strategy has succeeded at least in part and that the city dwellers have gained a wealth advantage. Lipton concurs with this view. Breman also maintains that, in Indonesia at least, the urban standard of living exceeds that of the countryside by far. 'Even the poorest people in Jakarta are probably much better off than the low-income strata in the villages of Java!' (1976, 1872). Proper comparison is hampered by the fact that in the city calculations are made with money wages, while in the rural area, with its self-sufficient peasants, estimates have to be used. Sen provides for this the rule that labour costs are arrived at by 'the rate of substitution between output and non-work that is acceptable to the labourer', or in case the decision lies with the head of the peasant family, 'the valuation is that of the head in question' (1975, 51). Comparisons of this kind, though perhaps theoretically defensible, are patently less convincing than when in both cases, in the city and in the countryside, the same standards are applied. Furthermore, it should be borne in mind that agricultural work is seasonal - an obvious point which nevertheless has aroused controversy among economists. Some think that the marginal value of agricultural labour, through overwork, has been nil, while others who observed labour shortages think the exact opposite. In the same sphere lies Jones's finding that seasonal labour shortages, caused by migration of especially the young to the cities, tend to become so acute in North India and West Pakistan that subsistence agriculture comes under severe pressure (1971). There is also a body of thought which argues that the so-called green revolution, in which high-yielding seed strains were introduced, has benefited disproportionately the more prosperous peasants, who could afford the necessary investment in fertilizer and irrigation works. It follows from this, incidentally, that the gap between urban and rural, which is equally deplored, has been narrowed.

However difficult it may be to document accurately and indisputably the skewed distribution of income, there remains a strong feeling that inequality persists - and for the present subject it is important to note that this influences the direction and scale of industrial projects.

TECHNOLOGY AND THE DETERMINATION OF INCOME

The purchasing power of high-income earners is directed, in the developing countries as elsewhere, to consumer goods in the luxury sphere. These have to be imported from the industrial countries. This will recoil upon the balance of payments, simply because the small foreign currency reserves would be better employed to import means of production. But if the latter are imported and then used to satisfy demands existing by virtue of a lopsided distribution of income, then the scarce means available are still employed misguidedly. Electric razors, refrigerators, deep freezers, cars and cosmetics are some examples of consumer goods which are available in the city shops but can only be bought by a privileged stratum. Such goods are manufactured by industrial methods, which, like the goods themselves, have been borrowed directly from the wealthy Western economies. The amount of labour required for their production is relatively insignificant, and minimal purchasing power is generated. The desired 'trickling-down effect' fails to materialize; no development can be expected from this consumption-directed investment. Le Brun reports for Latin America that 45 per cent of manufactured products and 74 per cent of durable goods are consumed by 5 per cent of the population (1973, 282).

In Africa the example of Kenya is interesting, because there a choice was made in favour of an almost unrestricted free-market economy, and poor countries which have pinned their hopes on the capitalist model of development are rare. Leys has rejected the strategy in emotive terms in his 'Political Economy of Neo-Capitalism'. After a decade of independence, the World Bank praised Kenya's growth performance. 'Virtually every indicator of performance in (the economic) field is well above average ... the gross domestic product grew at an average rate of about 7% between 1946 and 1972 ... real per capita incomes have increased significantly.' But once the initial industrial investments had worked through, progress came to a halt. In 1972 a report of the International Labour Office spoke of 'gross imbalances' and the World Bank has since also complained of shortcomings in distribution ('The Economist', 11 March 1978). In 1975 the Kenyan government introduced measures to ensure a more egalitarian development of incomes. The traditional policy instrument to achieve this has been progressive taxation. But in poor countries, with their limited and relatively shaky administrative apparatus and a commercial and industrial class relatively unfamiliar with the principles of book-keeping (or, alternatively, so thoroughly familiar as to administer them twice: once for the business and once for the taxman), it is difficult for any government to tax high-income groups effectively. In itself this encourages the consumption of luxury goods, since undeclared earnings are not reinvested, but used to buy expensive consumer goods. In 1972 the ILO advised the Kenyan government to freeze the incomes of top civil servants for a period of five years, and to use the funds thus released to raise, through specific projects, the incomes of the lowest class. The proposal was not carried out (ILO, 1972).

Direct taxes aimed at restricting consumption in the luxury sphere are, by contrast, very easily imposed. But it is more important to stop providing industrialists with incentives towards import substitution. Development plans should have a strong built-in preference for investment in productive capacity, which creates maximum employment and is directed to the utilitarian satisfaction of needs. This will have an effect on income distribution, since the relatively higher wages now paid in manufacturing industry depend on the capital-intensive technology applied there. A consciously chosen simple technology could therefore cause a fall in wages and thereby reduce differentials in the standard of living. Some observers have reported that the range of consumer goods for low-income groups includes more labour-intensively produced goods. If this is the case, then the three goals of the policy - creation of employment, spread of income and saving of capital - can be achieved in combination.

For Puerto Rico, however, the exact opposite is reported (Weisskoff et al., 1973). The familiar plastic sandals worn in tropical countries require greater capital investment, but are cheaper and longer-lasting than leather footwear. Bicycles and fertilizer, used extensively in rural areas, are produced by capital-intensive methods. By the same token, the rich do not only demand goods that are the result of large-scale industrial activity: clothing made to measure and specially designed furniture, for instance, provide a lot of work; in addition, the wealthy in these countries employ many servants. It is not easy to choose a technology that fulfils all the criteria derived from theory!

Although the ambitious target figures of the development decades proclaimed by the United Nations have not been achieved, an historical comparison with the growth rates of initial industrialization in the rich countries reveals that the rise in income in the Third World is not deficient.

The same cannot be said for the rise in purchasing power: on the assumption that this will be directed firstly to the undeniable 'basic need' of eating, the rise in food consumption is lagging far behind what is to be expected if the poorest have an equal share in the growing wealth.

This has in part been caused by the development strategy that has been adopted; for income is formed at industrial jobs, and their expansion has been hampered by the application of modern technology.

9 Alternatives

> 'There is a Gandhi solution for every Nkrumah solution.' (Stewart)

The alternative technologies which have been discussed in the preceding chapters have in large part an 'intermediate' character. Schumacher places them between 'the hoe and the tractor, or the panga and the combine harvester' (1975, 16). He considers the simpler device of each pair inadequate because economic growth is not possible with such primitive tools; the complex devices, however, are far too developed, they fit into a phase of technical and economic maturity which has not (yet) been reached in the situation under consideration. Cairncross believes that for the same reason certain American production methods are unsuitable for Europe in that they are too closely geared to high labour costs and a big market (1972, 111). A technology suited to European countries could be considered, from the standpoint of the American technical vanguard, as European, that is, adapted, in the same way that Nyerere considered the ox-drawn plough and not the tractor as Tanzanian, that is, adapted. It must be remembered here that the representation of the distribution of wealth in the world, which is talked of in terms of rich and poor countries and the gap between them, does not reflect reality wholly accurately. There is no 'gap' if all countries are ranked according to annual income per head. There are countries which are neither rich nor poor, but in a middle position economically. Consequently, the advocates of adaptation should have high hopes for an intermediate technology in these countries; but this line of argument is conspicuously absent in the literature. This is because even the writers opposing technology recognize implicitly that it is a wealth-generating factor. That is why Schumacher does not expect the poor peasant to cope with only a hoe and a panga, even though these tools are very 'organic'. Something better must be found; something that is more efficient, makes work easier and satisfies (for the time being very simple) needs. In some sense the most adapted technology is therefore slightly ahead of local time, as it were, and brings benefits without eroding the quality of life. The call for adapted technology is thus really one for a slight non-adaption!

THE DISAPPEARING MIDDLE

Van Bronckhorst mentions a 'Technology that makes it possible to change the present situation into a more desirable one' (1974, 13). The central feature of the kind of technology referred to here is expressed in the phrase of a technique being 'ahead of its time'. It is possible that eventually it will be caught up with, become contemporary and then obsolete. In the course of economic development, which of course occurs diachronically, an industrial activity which was once ahead - and used a modern technique - will be overtaken by a more modern technique. Schumpeter described this process in 1912 in his 'Theory of Economic Development'. In the modern theory of growth the mechanism under the heading 'leading sector' has played an important role. The provocative dictum: 'There is no alternative technology', which an annoyed engineer appended to his doctoral thesis, should in fact read 'There is but alternative technology'. All techniques which could be applied to manufacture a product are alternatives of each other; whichever is the most appropriate depends primarily on the stage of development of the economy at a certain point of time. Viewed in this way, the whole problem of adaptation becomes one of the transfer of a technology from an economically advanced country to an economically underdeveloped country. The process is aggravated, according to Schumacher, by what he calls 'the disappearing middle' ('Tool', 1967, 18). In bookshops, he elaborates, one can find the latest publications and the classics, but rarely anything from the intervening period. It is the same with technology. The older, more labour-intensive methods have disappeared and the machines have been scrapped.

THE DYNAMIC OF SECONDHAND EQUIPMENT

But they have not all been scrapped. A Filipino industrialist invested $ 10,000 in secondhand machines and produced so cheaply that a competing company in which $ 1,500,000 had been invested began to make losses. An Algerian razor-blade factory also produced far below the cost price of a modern installation elsewhere (Jéquier, 1976, 40). Such reports prompted the ILO to commission a study, within the framework of the World Employment Programme, into the jute-processing industry in Kenya, where both new and secondhand machines are in use. Both new and old were imported from Dundee. The spinning machines arrived in good condition and could be reinstalled with little difficulty. Their purchase price was low and the variable costs were roughly equivalent to those for the new machines. The cost reduction, due in particular to the small amounts to be written off for depreciation, was almost 43 per cent. The purchase price of secondhand weaving machines was considerably lower, but by the time they had been lifted, transported, reassembled, reinstalled and put in working order the cost advantage had evaporated. A new machine bought for 65,000 EA shillings cost once installed 120,000 EA shillings. An older machine, bought for 6,000 EA shillings cost reinstalled 40,000. Once the machines were in use the total running costs for the used machines turned out to be so much higher that unit production costs were eventually more than doubled (Cooper and Kaplinsky, 1974). Volkov sees in this an imperialist strategy to lumber the poor countries with outmoded secondhand equipment, and he reproaches his bourgeois colleague Kaldor for singing the praises of cast-offs (1975, 13).

Third World governments evidently also see it this way, since bans on imports of used tools and machines are quite common. But a careful evaluation of expected returns in every case is to be preferred. It is, though, not easy to make such an analysis. And with this element of uncertainty it is - quite apart from considerations of prestige, which also play their part - understandable that industrialists and planners would rather not risk investing in secondhand equipment. How an expected development - Smith would have spoken here of a hidden hand - could turn a disadvantage into an advantage was shown when a shortage of spare parts for machines which were no longer produced in the country of origin stimulated business for the local machine workshops. Singer is pleased with the 'learning processes through repair, maintenance and the copying of old designs' (1977, 59).

If through these experiences an indigenous capital-goods sector can be built up, then the path of many an industrialized country will be followed (as latterly by Japan, whose industrial apparatus is no cause for worry).

But the advocates of intermediate technology do not envisage such a capitalist future. One of the criteria they apply is that investment remains limited, and here too the intermediate position appears attractive. Schumacher's figures are admittedly presented as symbolic values but when he typified the technology applied in a poor country as a '£1 technology' and the industrial technology as a '£1,000 technology', then an investment of £100 for an adapted technology is clearly given an intermediate position (1974, 50). Dickson works with different numbers but does the same: for him the 'traditional workplace' cost £2, the modern £2,000 and the alternative £200 (1974, 151).

INVESTMENT INTENSITY

Now it is not necessary to work here with random numbers. Levels of investment per worker during the development of the industrial countries are roughly known; the figures are most meaningful when the sum invested is expressed in terms of the worker's wage. In the nineteenth century, investment per worker in British industry was equivalent to four months' wages, in France to six to eight months' wages. In 1953 this figure was in the American industry 29 months' wages. For developing countries the average is 350 months' wages (Uchendu, 1975, 189). For Indian industry it is as much as 600 months' wages (Jacob, 1976, 16). The unequal relationship during the transfer of a modern, large-scale technology to an infant industry in poor countries is glaringly obvious. Another approach assumes that annually one-twentieth of the available labour must be equipped with capital goods, while in the succeeding 19 years the remainder will have to be supplied with replacement capital goods. Assuming further that the savings ratio is 20 per cent and that one quarter of this is used for improvements in infrastructure, Stewart arrives (on the basis of the figures derived from the ILO Statistical Yearbook of 1971) at an investment per worker of $ 28,965 for the United States, $ 12,519 for Britain, $ 639 for Nigeria and $ 551 for India (1974, 19). This means that only about one-sixtieth of the sum available for the creation of one job in the US is available for the same purpose in India. There is, in other words, good cause, or rather, a compelling reason to choose a technology that requires the lowest possible investment. This is all the more essential in the case of production processes that require high levels of liquid capital - a consideration not included in the above scheme. Ramaer reports that in an electronics factory in Tanzania one million guilders were invested, of which fl.600,000 were in the building and fl.400,000 in machinery. Since 142 people were employed, the investment per worker was just over fl.7,000 - a relatively small sum. Besides this, however, the sums shown in Table 1 were booked in stocks and credits.

TABLE 1

Raw materials and parts transported by the parent company in Europe	fl.1 000 000
Raw materials and parts in warehouse	2 000 000
Raw materials and parts in use	500 000
Stocks of finished product	3 000 000
Trade credits advanced	2 000 000
Total	fl.8 500 000

The conduct of business, which was commenced with an investment of capital goods valued at fl.1,000,000, required in fact fl.9,500,000 or almost fl.67,000 per worker, almost ten times the modest capitalization per worker (1976, 7).

All kinds of goods can be produced using all kinds of techniques, requiring more or less capital, more or fewer jobs, more or fewer raw materials. They are each other's alternatives.

But in a concrete economic situation, where demand, available skills, supply and motivation of labour, and level of capitalization are known, there is really only one appropriate technology - namely the one that incurs the lowest cost per unit produced and sold.

As the parameters change - demand changes, wage rates go up, interest falls, knowledge widens - technical innovation comes into play. Manufacturers switch to a different, by their standards better, production method. Realizing that the variability created by a technique can procure them at least a temporary advantage, they put up the cost of research to accelerate the process of technical progress and direct it as they see fit.

Applied in an economic situation characterized by totally different parameters, such an innovation lacks all economic sense and also loses its wealth-generating effect. In this situation there is again but one alternative - but a different one - the most appropriate.

10 Contradictions and dependences

'Nothing is easier than to be radical for another country.' (Streeten)

Participants in the valium culture of present-day industrialism repudiate what they regard as the overdevelopment of a technicized society.

The poor countries should definitely not go along this road.

The 1930s' image of the industrial superpower as a malignant growth, then used to mark the stranglehold of trusts and cartels, is again conjured up, this time to indicate how that part of the world where all the factories are has dominated that part which supplies all their raw materials. The Third World was forced to become economically subservient. That road they must also depart from. But poverty cannot be eradicated without factories and in economic isolation. And poverty appears, from the view point of the welfare state, as an intolerable evil. To free themselves of abject poverty, the poor countries should, in this vision, turn down the road on which the rich countries have preceded them; but they should choose a technical apparatus which will be adequate for only part of the way. They should call a halt somewhere before the stage attained by the West. The best economy in this conception is a halfway economy.

CONFLICTING ENDS

A ratio commonly used in development economics is the capital coefficient, which is the proportion of the value of the capital goods employed in production to the value of the goods produced. If, for instance, an investment requires 12 million monetary units (Mu) and annual production is worth 4 million Mu, then the capital coefficient is 3. The lower this figure, the better, and vice versa. Mechanization forces down the capital coefficient, which therefore tends to fall as industrialization advances. If 100,000 Mu are available to start a small textile factory, and the capital coefficient is 2.5 and the technically required investment per worker is 1,000 Mu, then the investment will create 100 jobs and produce goods worth 40,000 Mu per year. If it is decided to do the spinning by hand, then the necessary investment per worker will be much lower, say 100 Mu, but the capital coefficient will be 5, less favourable. Now the available 100,000 Mu will provide 1,000 jobs, but the value of production per year will only be half, namely 20,000 Mu. Capital costs per unit of produced good are now higher. Here a conflict seems to arise between the goal of maximization of employment on the one hand and the goal of minimization of capital expenditure on the other. Yet these two are precisely the goals envisaged by alternative technology. At a NUFFIC conference in 1975 De Wilde defined its criteria as stimulation of employment and reduction of the capital requirements (1975, 1). Calculated per worker the latter is possible - per unit of product it is unlikely.

But there are other conflicts. At the conference it was also demanded that adapted technology should be simple, the operation of the machines should be understandable, maintenance should be easy to carry out. It is of course known - and deplored in alternative circles - that while mechanization has made all kinds of skills and training superfluous, the adjustment and maintenance of equipment which is otherwise simple to operate have become highly skilled. The greater the manual work in the production process, the greater the skills required; the less the manual work, the more is left to the machines, which in turn require more expert attention. At the end of technical development stands the robot, which can perform consistently the tasks for which it is programmed, but in the event of breakdown it can only be repaired by a highly skilled electronics engineer. One of the mainsprings of mechanization is the desire to simplify industrial management. As more people become involved in the production process, organization becomes more difficult. And precisely the countries we are concerned with lack, as has already been mentioned, the kind of experience and knowledge required to manage large workforces.

On the other hand, the idea - advocated above all by Schumacher - that industry should revert to small-scale operations is easily reconciled with a policy of employment creation. His London group is investigating techniques which are appropriate to cottage industries, where members of one family using tools worth a mere £20 produce goods for local use. Further research is being carried out into the organization of co-operatives, which, using means of production worth up to £100 can supply a whole region; and lastly into small-scale industry which uses more highly skilled labour and machines worth up to £500.

The setting-up of small enterprises in developing countries has been urged for a long time and has been studied in detail. Most experts are of the opinion that such small undertakings will indeed employ relatively more labour, which is also partly explained by higher interest rates, inaccessibility of subsidies, and the possibility open to small firms of evading social legislation which in effect puts up labour costs. The upshot of this is that the factor prices with which the small industrialist calculates, reflect more accurately the real scarcity relationships, and some economists consider this a sufficient reason to praise this state of affairs as 'healthy'. It remains to be seen whether development will continue in a 'healthy' manner - though it should be remembered that the big European and American conglomerates which began as small enterprises initially also had only slight chances of survival. An infant mortality rate for small firms of 90 per cent is quite normal. Only about the survivors will memorial volumes be published, however; the failed competitor will disappear from the annals of history after the announcement of his bankruptcy. People at British Leyland - a firm, incidentally, whose health has not improved with growth - remember fondly the bicycle shed in which Morris started his career. But of the hundreds of car manufacturers that have ever set up in business, only twelve giants, which now supply practically the whole market, have survived. The growth of the computer industry in the wake of one of the most recent technical breakthroughs shows that in this respect nothing has changed since the turn of the century: of the 70 enterprises set up between 1950 and 1965, less than a third were still in business in 1970 (Jéquier, 1976, 29).

Now 'small' in the United States will not mean the same as 'small' in Togo. The most commonly applied norm is not capitalization but size of workforce. The average for the 'small business' category is often put at 20 employees: it includes the tailor helped by some members of his family and a few employees; it also includes the man, assisted by two boys handing him the tools, welding car bodies together on the side of the road in a Javanese city. It includes the whole informal sector, about which so much has been written recently. In the countryside and in the backstreets, an economy has been discovered which had hitherto escaped attention, not indexed in the statistics.

Van Bronckhorst has called it very aptly the 'halfway economy' (1976). Here, in thousands of small workshops, a range of goods is produced which fulfils the requirements comprised in the 'basic needs' notion: production is attuned to local needs, cheap, and carried out with a minimum of aid and resources - but still more effective and technically more sophisticated than the primitive, traditional method of production. 'This informal sector represents a vast pool of technology', writes Jéquier respectfully, 'both in hardware and in software ... which plays an immensely important part in the economic system' (1976, 39). Here Schumacher's demand for the setting-up of workshops 'at source', that is, where people are living now, is fulfilled. Breman, who investigated the phenomenon in India, points to its function as 'nursery and train training ground for entrepreneurs' (1976, 1941). Hopes are pinned on this sector to spark the growth to a real, respectable small business sector. These publications and the considerably less sympathetic presentation of multinationals' activities sometimes leave the impression that local industry of somewhat larger proportions is practically non-existent. This is not the case, however. In fact more than half the labour force of manufacturing industry in the developing countries is employed in larger firms. In Iran, Colombia and Malaysia firms with about fifty employees employ 77, 71 and 40 per cent, respectively, of the total industrial labour force, and produce 59, 57 and 25 per cent of value added. Similar figures are reported for other developing countries for which data are available (Morawetz, 1974, 525).

Another aspect of the simple, local technology which deserves the attention of those interested in alternatives is its use of resources. A large factory is certainly not set up without due consideration of the availability of natural resources, but the demand for high, and in many cases also consistent, quality is inherent in the mechanized production process, while simpler tools allow greater latitude. Not only industrial equipment, but also the end product is determined, in its constituent parts, by other demands than the ones that can be traced to local conditions. Thus in Kenya large amounts of corrugated iron sheets have been imported for roof construction. Traditional local roofing is ignored. Plastic is used widely where wood or bamboo, locally available, would suffice. The informal sector, which approximates more closely to the traditional methods of production, will be more readily inclined to resort to traditional and hence locally available materials. It is not assured that this method of production will create more employment, but at least investments are spread wider in the sense that local resources are tapped, so that at any rate in the areas where they are found jobs will be created. And it is also much more likely that the local workshops will be able to manufacture the kind of tools which a simpler technology requires; the chances for the emergence of an indigenous capital-goods industry will increase accordingly. In the meantime, however, some doubts have been raised. The popular recommendation to manufacture 'adapted goods' apparently springs from the idea that invariably adapted techniques will be used in their production. For traditional tools this may still hold, but the plastic sandal mentioned earlier is certainly adapted, though its production is anything but labour-intensive. It is also possible that utterly unadapted goods are made for export using very labour-intensive methods. A rejection of this would be not so much a choice of economic policy as a political-economic choice. A trend in this direction is clearly evident in the discussion of alternative technology.

'The developing countries believe, in a strongly ideologically coloured analysis, that they have uncovered a scene of worldwide technological exploitation' (Wegener, 1976, 531). The dogma of dependence has, judging by the number of its adherents, become an important movement in the developing countries in recent years. And the various schools within it display strong dislike of the private-capitalist mode of production. Dislike of any kind of dependence felt by peoples whom the West has subjugated in some cases for centuries is, of course, quite understandable.

CONFLICTING INTERESTS

Yet, for a detached discussion it is important to determine what exactly is meant by this infamous dependence. Stewart considers the concept 'not susceptible of rigorous definition' (1977, 116). She defines the absence of 'scientific and innovative capacity' as one of the causes of dependence, and adds that it can also be seen as one of its symptoms. Elsewhere in the literature this leaning towards tautology can also be discerned: the poor countries are poor because they are dependent, and because they are dependent they are poor. Now there is something to be said for this. We are following here the well-travelled theoretical path of vicious circles, in which Nurkse showed the way when he said very simply that 'A country is poor because it is poor'. When income is low, it is difficult to save, and so it will be difficult to partake of the benefits of so-called roundabout production. However, the immutability of the circular condition is contradicted by the historical circumstance that a number of once-poor countries have become less poor and even rich. Bauer therefore calls the vicious circle a myth. The essence of the dependence concept is, however, that the now-rich countries attained their wealth on the backs of the countries which are (and have remained) poor, and that the wealth of the few is conditional upon the poverty of the many. This argument appeals emotionally to our post-colonial sense of guilt. It also means that traditional - or let us not mince words: bourgeois - theory is guilty of bad faith when it pretends that it is just as easy to get rich in a rich world as it was to get rich in a poor world. Then again: 'Economic development and underdevelopment are the opposite faces of the same coin. Both are the necessary result and contemporary manifestation of internal contradictions in the world capitalist system. Economic development and underdevelopment are not just relative and quantitative, in that one represents more development than the other; economic development and underdevelopment are relational and qualitative, in that each is structurally different from, yet caused by, its relation with the other. Yet development and underdevelopment are the same in that they are the product of a single, but dialectically contradictory, economic structure and process of capitalism. One and the same historical process of the expansion of capitalism throughout the world has simultaneously generated - and continues to generate - both economic development and structural underdevelopment' (Frank, 1976, 9).

Some followers of the dependence school stay close to home, with Marx. They argue that the capitalist mode of production had to spread over the whole world in the 'last stage of the system'. Luxemburg saw in this, as we know, the necessary survival of the system, or to put it more accurately, the delay of its inevitable collapse. Warren, for instance, still believes that the poor countries will inevitably first have to develop in a capitalist direction before they can pass into a socialist stage. Others, like Frank, argue that the existence of dependence precludes the emulation of capitalist development. In the present circumstances, then, the poor countries can really only get poorer - 'immiserization'.

This does indeed seem the consequence of this particular view, even though in a number of countries actual events have called this into question. Consequently, opinions range from those of Furtado, Sunkel and Dos Santos, who are inclined to assume a stagnation, to Cardoso, who sees a chance of some marginal growth, though always in a subservient role (Lall, 1975, 807).

Van Nieuwenhuijze uses the popular argument that the modern world is characterized by a great mutual dependence of all countries (1976, 524). This is certainly true in an economic respect and it is indicated by the emergence of trade communities of previously competing countries. Governments are so conscious of interdependence that sometimes they recommend neighbouring countries to pursue certain economic policies because they expect beneficial repercussions on their own economies. In the stagnating, or rather stagflating, situation which arose in the industrial economies after 1973, the so-called 'locomotive' theory gained ground, which exhorted countries like West Germany and the United States not to shirk their responsibilities towards the other industrial countries dependent on them. The dependence theory described above is not affected by this: firstly because the poor countries have also experienced the detrimental effects of the industrial-economic recession as the market for their raw materials shrinks and their migrant workers are sent home; and secondly because the situation analysed in the theory is one of a much more overbearing dominance than tends to occur between relatively developed economies. In the latter case, dominated countries will react quickly to an imbalance of investment. Thus the French fear of 'coca-colonization' was vociferously expressed in Servan-Schreiber's 'Le Défit Americain' - which in the meantime has been taken up successfully: American investments are relatively less important in Europe than they were ten years ago ('The Economist', 4 February 1978, 78). In fact, the flow of investment from the European countries to the US has increased significantly.

Seen in this light, the potential damage which can be caused by economic dependence is limited by the ability of the victim to retaliate. Among the economically strong, this leads to a recovery of symmetry and the maintenance of mutual advantage. The literature of dependence arranges countries in two, economically very distinct categories: the rich and dominant countries; and the poor, above all the non-socialist, dominated countries. Here perhaps the tautological definition, which sees dependency as constituted by underdevelopment, comes home to roost. The abyss between poor and rich is not as yawning as television commentators like to think. There is a certain continuity of degrees of dependence, so that a small, rich country like the Netherlands may have a smaller say in European economic affairs than a poorer country like Brazil has in Latin America. Technical dependence is perhaps the most crippling component of economic dependence. Here too, though, the smaller rich countries suffer. The weak negotiating position accorded to the Third World in relation to the multinationals applies apparently also for some European countries in relation to Hoffman la Roche and its differential pricing policy for the indispensable valium. In terms of the number of patents granted abroad, Belgium is more dependent than India; and in terms of the level of foreign investment, Canada is more dependent than Brazil (Lall, 1975, 802).

The most concrete index of technological dependence seems to be provided by a costing of the transfer of technology from one country to another. Some estimates made along these lines have already been mentioned: according to UNCTAD, the aggregate cost of patents, licences, trade marks, management consultancy and technical advice amounted to $ 1,500 million in 1968, or 0.5 per cent of GNP. The uncertainties attached to these estimates are exacerbated by the fact that the costs of the technology may be included in the price of the machines, spare parts or raw materials, or even in the salaries of foreign advisers. Certain restrictions imposed by a contract may prevent the choice of cheaper alternatives and thus form in some sense (opportunity) costs. The crucial factor in the determination of technical dependence is whether, as in the relationship between industrial countries in which each can boast of certain technical skills, a compensating flow of technology can be discerned. If this is altogether absent, then the economic relationship will be very one-sided; and to maintain a balance, increased exports will have to relieve the balance of payments. The negotiating position of such a country is exceptionally weak. This of course need not be a total disaster for debtor countries, because big debts confer a degree of power over the creditor country, which must be mindful of a financial collapse of its debtors. Negotiating about technology presupposes knowledge, however, not only of the specific matters at hand but also of alternatives, of other processes - and in a wholly dependent country this knowledge will be absent. Nationalizations may successfully combat direct influence; but technical dictatorship is much more difficult to oppose. Only when a base of technical skills has been built up locally can control be regained.

Once an indigenous technical capacity exists, it is possible to bring production processes in line with a wider economic goal, which apart from an ambition to create wealth may be inspired by the desire for its equitable distribution among the population.

Good intentions do not always ensure good results. To create jobs, there must be present a supply of labour with a degree of training and a management able to supervise the increasing number of staff. An underdeveloped country is at a loss here. Moreover, it seems that the goal of saving capital can have an unfavourable effect on the capital coefficient.

The so-called informal sector corresponds to the concept of the halfway economy which development technologists aim for. The demand of dispersal is fulfilled here. Local materials are used. Production is directed to the satisfaction of *basic* needs.

This sector also avoids the technical-juridical tributes of patents and licences. And the increase of income reaches a broad section of the population. A lot is to be said for all these things.

11 Unemployment and idleness

'The white man knows how to make everything, but he does not know how to distribute it.' (Sitting Bull)

It has been pointed out years ago that the creation of employment must be the primary aim of development. 'Of all evils, worklessness is the worst' (Stewart and Streeten, 1971). Those who subscribe to this view will encounter throughout the world, but above all in the Third World, much that is to be lamented. Even in places where industrialization is making headway and where yields in agriculture have been improved, rising unemployment is reported, in particular in the urban areas. The number of unemployable persons grows in every economy in which investments do not create enough jobs to absorb the growing labour force. The evil is, as always, unequally divided: certain skills remain in great demand, and people who do not possess them are passed over; other skills become superfluous and people who possessed them are expelled. Certain age groups are included in the production process, others are not.

EMPLOYMENT

In countries with little industry and a rapidly growing population the problem of inclusion is that much greater. Let us assume that 20 per cent of the labour force is employed in industry. At an annual rate of increase of the labour force of 3 per cent, 15 per cent more jobs will have to be created in industry if the new supply on the labour market is to be absorbed. And if funds are invested in improved machines - which means almost invariably labour-saving machines - the expansion will have to be that much greater. The International Labour Office computed the number of jobs required in the poor countries during the 1970s at 300 million. In 1970 about two-thirds of the world labour force lived in the economically underdeveloped areas, and the number of jobs that need to be created there is double that in the rich countries. Data from the same ILO report show the extent to which the relative size of the population and the demographic growth rate combine to increase the potential supply of labour: from 1950 to 1960 it rose by 17 per cent (in the developed countries by 10.9 per cent); from 1960 to 1970 by 22.7 per cent (11.4 per cent); from 1970 to 1980 by 25 per cent (10.3 per cent). In Europe alone the increase is estimated for the last ten years at only 5.1 per cent, against for instance 28.8 per cent in Latin America (ILO, 1971). It must be remembered here that the industrial base of the poor countries is still small. In the years of incipient industrialization the presently wealthy countries had to cope with yearly growth rates of the labour force of between 1 and 1.5 per cent - a rather more simple task.

The question how this growing population is to be fed has long been a matter for discussion; the recently mooted problem of employment for all these people turns out to be equally difficult to solve. Even an effective demographic policy will bring alleviation only in the long run. Now it is worth noting that, still according to the Geneva report, the registered reserve of labour has shown little tendency to rise.

Sen remarks that in the calculation of unemployment figures something seems to escape the measuring rod of the statistician (1975, 49). The whole concept of being unemployed is inherent in a society in which there is something wrong with the labour market: the idea became the vogue during the European-American economic crisis of the 1930s. Where the supply of and demand for wage labour - labour paid on the basis of certain agreements - do not meet in the 'market place', there can be, in that sense, no unemployment. It is then still quite possible that all kinds of people have nothing to do. A person who is workless, as opposed to being unemployed, is someone who has absolutely nothing to do. '(Being) sprawled out in front of the television (is) as near to complete idleness as one can get without actually being unconscious' (Stewart, 1974, 34). The example shows that the phenomenon occurs also, or rather, precisely in industrial society: for there one can indulge in the luxury of spending, after eight hours of wage labour, the rest of the day in idleness, because income is sufficient to buy all the goods necessary for the maintenance of life. He who must forgo that income because he can find no paid

TABLE 2 Open unemployment rates in selected countries based on sample survey data, 1960-70[1] (percentage of labour force)

	1960	1961	1962	1963
Developing countries				
Argentina (Gran Buenos Aires)[3]	-	-	-	-
Chile	-	-	-	-
Chile (Gran Santiago)[3]	7.4	6.7	5.3	5.1
China	-	-	-	5.3*
Colombia (Bogota)[3]	-	-	-	7.9
Egypt	4.8*	3.2*	1.8*	-
Korea	-	-	8.4	8.1
Panama	-	-	-	5.8*
Philippines	6.3*	7.5	8.0	6.3
Syria	-	8.5*	6.0*	10.6*
Trinidad and Tobago	-	-	-	-
Venezuela	-	-	-	-
Developed countries				
Canada	7.0	7.1	5.9	5.5
Italy	4.2	3.5	3.0	2.5
Japan	1.1	1.0	0.9	0.9
Sweden	-	-	1.5*	1.7*
United States	5.5	6.7	5.5	5.7

Sources: International Labour Office, 'Year Book of Labour Statistics' (Geneva, 1970 and 1971).

1 Asterisks refer to different months from elsewhere in the series.
2 Arithmetic average of the years for which there are data.
3 Only the urban area.
4 Provisional.
5 Sampling design revised.
6 Slightly different coverage from the rest of the series.

1964	1965	1966	1967	1968	1969	1970	Average[2]
5.7*	5.3	5.6	6.4	5.0	4.3[4]	-	5.4
-	-	5.7*	4.7*	4.8	4.7*	3.4	4.7
5.3	5.4	5.4	6.1	6.0	6.2	7.1	6.0
4.4	3.4	3.1	2.3	1.7	1.9	1.7	3.0
7.1	8.9	10.1	12.2	11.5	9.6	8.1	9.4
1.9	-	-	-	3.1	-	-	3.0
7.7	7.4	7.1	6.2	5.1	4.8	4.5	6.6
7.4*	7.6	5.1	6.2	6.9	6.5	6.4	6.5
6.4*	7.2	7.3	8.0	7.8	6.7*	-	7.1
11.4*	7.4*	5.5*	5.3	7.4	4.3	-	7.4
-	14.0	14.0	15.0	15.0	13.5	-	14.3
-	-	-	7.7*	6.3*	6.5*	6.5	6.7
4.7	3.9	3.6	4.1	4.8	4.7	5.9	5.2
2.7	3.6	3.9	3.5	3.5	3.4	3.1	3.1
0.8	0.8	0.9	1.3[5]	1.2	1.1	1.2	1.0
1.6	1.2	1.6	2.1	2.2	1.9	1.5	1.7
5.2	4.5	3.8	3.8	3.6	3.5	4.9	4.8

employment is unemployed. He is thus in an exceptional position for which he can blame 'the system'. He who has no work in an agricultural society with a few cities and a few factories is not in the same sense unemployed.

I have contended elsewhere that the bush negro who cultivates his little plot on the edge of the Surinam river does not belong in the unemployment statistics computed in the capital (Duller, 1973). Yet in the literature of development economics one can detect a tendency to regard everyone who is not included in the 'modern sector' as unemployed, and therefore as a member of a potential reserve of labour for this sector. Because it was rather difficult to uphold the idea that, consequently, the majority of the population did nothing at all, the concept of 'hidden unemployment' - also invented in the 1930s to denote those persons who survived on the streets in the big, crisis-ridden cities by selling matches or baskets of strawberries - was taken up as an apt classification. What is indicated is that the person may well be active, but that his activity yields no positive value.

According to Nurkse, who was one of the first to apply the concept to the problem of development, there are in the countryside countless people who could be easily done away with in agriculture; no tears should be shed for their departure, indeed, agricultural production would not even decline. The marginal value of their labour was, said Nurkse, equal to nil (1953, 32). This led some to conclude that the withdrawal of this labour from the agricultural sector would in itself constitute, in economic terms, a very valuable act, since, whatever else people would do, the value of their activities could never be less than nil. Apart from Nurkse, Lewis and Rosenstein-Rodan also pleaded for the application of this hitherto hidden source of wealth in order to 'form capital' and thus supply the missing ingredient to spark off economic development. The wage which the formerly hidden unemployed were going to earn would be spent largely on foodstuffs that were being produced in the same quantities as before. Prices would rise and the peasant's income would also rise as a result of this miraculous intervention. Governments were handed on a plate the solution to the problem of development. Mellor and Stevens, Sarkar, Mehra, Sanghoi and the International Labour Office supplied the empirical data to underpin the vision: everywhere work was being done by ten people which could as easily have been done by five.

But Oshima, Hansen, Jorgensen and Schulz found evidence to the contrary (Sen, 1975, 32ff.). It was noticeable that small peasants who cultivated their little plots of land more intensively also had the greater yields. Schulz calculated that a flu epidemic in India adversely affected harvesting: the dead were missed after all, they had not toiled in vain when they were alive. In some cases it was observed that for certain seasonal activities there was a shortage of labour rather than a surplus. And finally, it should be mentioned that it is not improbable that surpluses of labour indeed exist in some countries, or even in some regions, and not in others. Or, as Uchendu ascertained, that certain improvements which brought an expansion of productive capacity in one area caused bottlenecks elsewhere in the economy, and that these required the commitment of all available labour (1975, 185).

COMPENSATION

Here the phenomenon appears which economists who are worried about the expulsion of labour by mechanization call the compensation mechanism. Approached from the cost side, compensating employment can occur in the capital-goods industry, which will book orders for the construction of new machines and can to this purpose use the labour which has become superfluous after the introduction of those machines elsewhere. For countries with their own heavy industry the objection can be raised that, firstly, the theory ignores the fact that the process occurs through time, and, secondly, that it assumes that the labour-saving machines have been completed at the very moment when the labour on location becomes redundant. For the developing countries the objection can be raised that the theory ignores that on the whole they cannot put the modern machines together themselves, so that superfluous labour for the completion of machine orders can at best be employed as immigrant labour in an industrial country. For both the poor and the rich countries the point must be made that labour is presented here as homogeneous while in actual fact the labour market is composed of many segment markets, as many as there are occupations. And in these segments shortages and surpluses can at times occur. It is not only doubtful, it is improbable, that welders who were made redundant after the installation of a welding machine can contribute to the construction of other welding machines. Forbes reports from the history of industry that the early machine designers had the greatest difficulty in recruiting labour with the required level of training and skills. 'Only too often parts refused to work after they had been put together. Watt found that cylinders made by the best workmen available in Glasgow varied 3/8 of an inch in diameter and Smeaton told that neither tools nor workmen existed that could manufacture so complex a machine with sufficient precision' (1968, 241). These problems occur in countries where industry is new and industrial labour is inexperienced. That the mechanism of compensation will be salutary is therefore not very likely.

But another compensation is provided via the determination of income: the goods produced by the new machines should be lower in price, so that the real income of the consumers rises. They can now spend part of their income on other goods. If the production of these requires more labour, then compensation will occur. This line of argument is also redolent of the flowing curves of the graphs which decorate the economics textbooks. Falling prices of perfect competition and collective demand curves shifted to the right do not give the impression of an accurate description of the economic reality of developing countries.

The positive appreciation of labour which, sometimes implicitly, lies at the root of many analyses, also seems not wholly applicable. The familiar expression of idleness being the parent of vice is echoed in Schumacher: 'Even poorly paid and relatively unproductive work is better than idleness' (n.d., 12). The thought that labour 'makes free'; that man 'posits himself in labour'; that maturity can only be properly reached in labour - in which the relationship to nature and fellow are determined - is a trait of Western culture. It has (as the above religious, existentialist and marxist phraseology indicates) influenced many different groups. 'Puritanism is a package deal', write Stewart and Streeten, and they are of the opinion that this package should not be unpalatable to those keen on development (1971, 152). Sen distinguishes besides the production aspect and the income aspect the 'Recognition aspect: employment gives a person the recognition of being engaged in something worth his while' (1975, 4). The theoreticians of 'alienation' dispute with vehemence that such feelings of belonging extend to industrial labour. Merens-Riedstra and Stroink, on the other hand, though referring to the opportunities of self-development and social recognition offered in labour, call the attitude 'learned and compulsively over-valued' and see the frustration of the redundant as the 'spiritual problem of unemployment' (1972, 281). It is again clear that we encounter here a cultural trait, relative like all the others: one cannot be certain whether it is a necessary condition for development. Weeks proves himself a realist when he notes that the emphasis put on employment has until now led primarily to 'faster growth of the foreign-owned modern sector' and that here lies, far from its solution, the problem itself (1971, 12).

What matters to the person looking for work is income. The creation of more jobs leads to a spreading of income over the growing number of participants in the production process. Morawetz calculates that the $ 100 million invested in the Colombian petrochemical industry, creating 2,500 jobs directly and another 3,500 indirectly, would, had it been invested in a labour-intensive industry, have provided work for 50,000 directly and 100,000 to 150,000 indirectly (1974, 50). This last figure becomes even more significant in the light of the fact that all Colombian firms with more than five employees employ in total only 350,000 workers.

For the Indonesian cigarette industry it has been calculated that fully automated production methods would provide 3,000 jobs, partly automated methods would provide 6,000 jobs, and labour-intensive methods would provide more than 40,000 jobs. Similar conclusions apply to other industries, as shown in Table 3 (Timmer et al., 1975, 73).

Legend has it that an emperor of ancient Greece was once shown a design for a machine which would be able to do the work of countless lsaves; he was most displeased by it: for what would become of the poor slaves? In the modern zeal to modernize, this aspect has at times receded into the background. As an employee of the World Bank put it: 'The chapter on employment strategy was always added at the end to round off the plans and make them look complete and respectable' (Haq, 1971, 10). In recent years the emphasis has shifted; many who want to help the poorest among poor assert that the first thing they should be provided with is work. In the radical vision this is best achieved by a revolutionary redistribution of power, where the national elite and the multinationals are ousted from their positions and the Chinese example is emulated, though in socio-cultural terms this country is no less further removed from Asia, Africa and Latin America than the Western industrial nations. But then the self-sufficiency and economic independence which the Chinese strive for have a wide appeal. In fact, during the 1950s the country received Russian aid, to which Dernberger partly attributes the economic growth of that period (1974, 237). Between 1952 and 1958 18.7 per cent of China's capital reserves consisted of industrial machinery, of which 28.1 per cent was imported. Ekstein estimates that the growth rate over the first five-year

TABLE 3 The workforce required in a number of industries using various techniques

Technology	cigarettes	flashlight batteries	soft drinks	tyres	plastic sandals
Capital-intensive	3,009	464	279		230
Intermediate	6,018	1,392	698	1,207	920
Labour-intensive	40,120	5,568	6,417	7,100	

plan (1953-7) would have been 20 to 50 per cent lower if China had not been able to import capital goods (1966, 123). The Soviet Union supplied whole factory installations; between 1950 and 1956 205 of these projects were completed and in the years 1958 and 1959 another 125. At that time 1,000 Russian engineers, most of them involved in the transfer of technology, were working in China.

The Chinese 'model of development' refers not so much to this period as to the succeeding one in which the country turned away from Russian influence in order to go forward and stand on its own (two) legs, a view which coincidentally dovetails into the popular Western image of self-activity, as documented in the many tomes on 'self-sufficiency' on sale in the bookshop of Schumacher's London group. The aim of small production units using simple tools and machines ('let a hundred flowers blossom') fits in marvellously well with the preference for alternative technologies which the said group shares with others of its ilk. The small iron foundries in the countryside, which at the time were much discussed, were classic examples of small-scale technologies. They were given up for an equally classic reason: the quality of the product left much to be desired (Stewart, 1972, 119).

The so-called self-reliance model seems further relevant because during the era of Chairman Mao attempts were made to overcome the 'three differences', that is, the differences in economic growth between industry and agriculture, in the status between intellectual labour and manual labour, and between urban and rural wealth (Rifkin, 1975, 263). The development strategy followed is known as 'walking on two legs' and the setting-up of small labour-intensive firms was encouraged throughout the country. Not surprisingly, Bhalla observes that there is no unemployment in China, even if productivity is at times 'sub-optimal' (1974, 65). It is as yet not clear whether the Chinese strategy will remain unchanged. In the autumn of 1977 the new Politburo published a declaration from which it can be deduced that the new Helmsman, Hua, is as 'The Times' puts it, more interested in 'results than ideology' (13 September 1977). Now China had been buying in the United States ever since 1973, at a value of some $ 10 million per year, and the declaration mentioned above proclaimed that 'only the most decadent and reactionary ruling classes close their doors and reject any good things from other lands'. China now desired 'advanced technology, not to hinder but to promote our own creativeness, not to weaken but to increase our ability to develop our national economy'. Towards the end of 1977 'The Economist' sent some journalists to China, who, to their surprise, found they were being reproached for 'Western unwillingness to sell China its most advanced technology' ('The Economist', China Survey, 31 December 1977, 23).

At the opposite end of the political spectrum there is the school which expects salvation in the determination of prices on free markets. The excessive use of capital and the restricted use of labour is, as explained earlier, here attributed to price distortion. Once this is counteracted by the appropriate measures, the restoration of what are referred to in this circle as 'healthy conditions' is assured. The now cheap labour will flow towards the firms managed by free entrepreneurs burgeoning with initiative. They will be most economical with the factor capital. Import licences will have to be abolished, subsidies will have to be curtailed, and government interference ended. Since the hypothesis of perfect markets, perfect market knowledge, and reliability of present prices - even if they represent to a greater extent 'balance' - has not been fulfilled as the guideline for future developments, the approach is largely an academic one. An active economic policy which offers incentives that lead to a factor choice giving priority to employment - and thus the formation of income - is to be preferred.

Recent economic history has contradicted the view that labour is an easily accessible source of wealth (which is, moreover, self-reproducing) and that through it the growth process can be set in motion.

In the era of full employment in the industrial countries (which has come to an end only recently!) the view could arise which recommended the exhaustion of the labour reserves as an effective development strategy.

Demography has had a sobering effect.

And the compensation mechanisms which, operating through redeployment of labour, were believed to balance redundancy in one place by expansion of employment elsewhere, have turned out to be less efficacious than theory assumed.

In adapted, intermediate technology the economic strategist encounters a means which will optimize employment for a given investment.

12 Productivity

'The mercantile economy seems to consider production and not consumption as the end of all industry and commerce.' (Adam Smith)

In an area where so many have a political axe to grind it is useful to define clearly the goal dictated by economic considerations: what matters is income. In the 1930s Keynes proposed rather cynically that people should dig holes and then fill them in again. In many tropical countries there is indeed a tradition of involving large numbers of people in the execution of certain tasks; the plentiful domestic staff, already deemed unproductive by Adam Smith in the England of his day, is a good example of this, but in commerce and industry it is also often the case that more labour is employed than is absolutely necessary. An inclination, or even a social obligation, to allow even the most remote members of the extended family to share in this way apparently forces the wealthy into this behaviour, while in addition they can affirm their social status through it. Here Keynes's solution is not applicable after all, since there is no idle industrial apparatus which only needs the incentive of effective demand to swell the flow of goods and bring supply in line with demand. Merely employing more labour does not increase real income, as the British trade unions have discovered.

PERFORMANCE

If, as Rees-Mogg calculated, 'one Dutch man hour = two British man hours', then consequently real income in Britain can only be half that in the Netherlands ('The Times', 28 September 1977). As a matter of fact, on 13 February 1665 Samuel Pepys noted in his diary 'how despicably (the Dutch) speak of us for using so many hands more to do anything they do, they closing a cable with twenty that we use sixty men upon'. An extreme solution to the problem of distribution consists of allocating incomes irrespective of participation in the process of production. Accustomed as we are to the link between performance and income, in discussions of distribution we tend to concentrate on employment creation. The idea is given additional support by the positive evaluation of the phenomenon of labour and by the less frequently expressed belief that incentive and performance are positively correlated, as is instanced by the familiar image of the donkey and the carrot. Yet one can envisage how in a highly developed stage of industry certain groups, less susceptible to incentive, will not or perhaps only belatedly participate in production, or perhaps will be withdrawn from it at a less advanced age. In fact the industrial revolution has throughout been accompanied by compulsory education, the raising of the school-leaving age, fixed working hours, reduction of the working week, retirement and early retirement. In recent years the notion of 'work sharing' has been appended to this list: a full job is divided up between several people. 'Increasingly', Galbraith observes, 'the purpose of the economy has become not the goods it produces, but the jobs it provides' (1971, 5). Sen, writing about a less matured phase of prosperity, calls employment one of the less refined methods of distributing income (1975, 84).

This is certainly true and provides the justification for all kinds of mitigating and corrective transfers of income in the countries which can afford to carry them through. But this is not the crux of the development problem. The crux is that there is not enough to share to begin with. The distribution problem only arises when there is something to distribute. The critics of the green revolution were disaffected because the bigger harvests as a result of new seed strains have benefited the rich peasants more than the poor. But if these new strains had not been developed, food production would not have gone up either, and everyone would have been as badly off as before - hardly a satisfying thought. The point is to intervene in such a way that the created surplus directly reaches those most in need.

For a long time it was thought that this would occur by itself; as explained earlier, the talk was then of the 'trickling down' of wealth which, as production expands, labour becomes more scarce and the unions more powerful, will gradually extend to the materially less well endowed. Indian agronomists like Swaminathan and Jain have indeed suggested that the green revolution will in the long run also move in this direction ('The Economist', 13 May 1978, 107). The objection to be made is regarding the non-committal nature of the 'in the long run', hence the strong emphasis which the International Labour Office has latterly put on the immediate creation of employment.

LINKAGE

A reference was already made earlier to the phenomenon of the so-called 'linkage', which Hirschman postulated as the great lever in his theory of development, dealing with the effects of an initial investment on income and capacity. Every kind of economic activity sparked off by an initial investment leads potentially to the stepping-up of production elsewhere, and in this view a development strategy needs to be geared to the maximization of these effects.

If one imagines an industry as a chain of enterprises successively using each other's end products as raw materials for further production, until the final product reaches the consumer, then in Hirschman's vision an investment done in the middle area will yield the greatest 'linkage'. Expansion of capacity there will mean that the previous stages can count on an increased demand for their goods. The consequent fall in price will also have a stimulating effect on the higher echelons of the industry. Thus far the model is rather simple. It becomes more complex, however, when employment creation is given priority: it is after all uncertain whether the secondary investments will fulfil this criterion. Morawetz speaks lightheartedly of 'ancillary activities', such as packing, storing and handling materials, which provide greater scope for labour-intensive methods (1974, 520). Any projects involving the moving of earth - road or dam construction, for instance - are pre-eminently the activities which could give work to large numbers of people. But lorries and bulldozers can do the job just as well, and in the construction of the Bhakra Mangal dam in India even conveyor-belts were used.

The engineers pointed to the costs, which would have been 20 per cent higher if exclusively unskilled labour equipped with picks and shovels had been deployed. Shonfield, however, reported that the engineers had no desire to see 'thousands of primitive and probably half-starved Indians crawling all over their site' (1960, 15).

Employment can be further eroded when an investment leads to the growth of sales and fall in price of a commodity which local industry has previously been competing with. The plastic sandals which cheaply meet the need for footwear in tropical countries enter into competition with sandal-makers who satisfy this need with locally available materials and by labour-intensive methods. The International Labour Office has conducted an investigation into the effects on employment of the modernization of the textile sector in Indonesia. It turned out that, though in the period between 1966 and 1971 86,000 jobs had been created in textiles, at the same time 410,000 jobs had been lost (1973).

AMBAR CHARKA

It is evident that the choice of technology is of preponderant influence on such an outcome. The choice largely determines the resultant labour productivity. It tends to be low in the traditional method of production, high in the modern method. The first situation is not desirable because it is responsible for the low level of production and thus the situation of underdevelopment; the latter is unsuitable because of its inadequate use of labour. Intermediate technology therefore lies indeed somewhere in the middle: it is more efficient than the traditional and it improves labour productivity without reaching the point where the erosion of employment begins to dominate. This also means that, as is evident in the case of the construction of the dam, a cost advantage will have to be forgone. It was shown a long time ago that the *ambar charka*, an improved handloom for cottage industry, cost both more labour and more capital compared to the modern spinning machine. Furthermore, cottage industry is exempt from tax. Had the textile industry been set up on a large scale, then the consumer would have paid a lower price for his clothing while the additional tax revenue has been estimated at $ 32 million ('The Economist', 13 May 1978). Yet the small-scale sector employs two and a half times as many people as modern industry - some 10 million people in textiles alone. And there are other, less quantifiable advantages. India knows no dole system, and in some sense the lower tax revenue is the sacrifice made in the place of social benefits which in other countries are funded through the state budget. Industrialization also means urbanization, and that means, if social costs are to be avoided, roads, housing and sewage systems to provide for the needs of factory workers. Where these facilities are not provided, slums arise, and that these are social disasters is beyond argument. Cottage industry in the countryside provides housing without additional expense. The relatively low density of the population makes the other facilities unnecessary. The problem of transporting goods around a large country is reduced, because cottage industries are located nearer to their markets. Under these circumstances a simple, machine-powered spinning machine can compete with a factory and a reasonable profit is assured. An improved loom enables the weaver to earn three and a half times more than he could earn on a pit loom. 'The Economist', hardly a journal to throw itself away on half-baked social experiments, concludes that 'small can be made beautiful enough for millions to get a living from it' (13 May 1978, 112).

Throughout the preceding discussion, differences in productivity have been reduced to their most significant cause: differences in the technology applied. The perfection of technology raises productivity, and because the results of this advance do not manifest themselves everywhere simultaneously, divergences arise which are sometimes so striking that some authors have been persuaded to suggest a duality in the forms of economic activity: technological dualism.

ENCLAVE

A sharp contradiction arises when a technique developed in the industrial countries which aims at maximum productivity is transferred to an economy which is otherwise characterized by simple production techniques and low labour productivity.

The penetration of modern technology in disregard - or rather, in absence - of the effects on other economic activity evokes the image of the enclave. If the investments originate from foreign funds and are managed from abroad, they can justly be considered an extension of the industrial economy of the rich countries, investments undertaken to increase their own wealth and only in the second instance, if at all, to serve the economic interests of the undeveloped country.

The differences are thrown into relief by the unique appearance of the enclave. Discrepancies in wealth become more glaring as the physical distance between rich and poor is shortened. That is why visitors to the poor countries are struck by the contrast between the elegant city centre and the adjoining slum quarters. Thus the Western industrial sector too is a disruptive factor in an area of poverty and low productivity. But the outcomes of wealth measurements at a distance, across the borders of even adjacent countries, are no less divergent.

In 1967 the Nederlands Economisch Instituut found that in Mexico industrial productivity was 17 per cent of that in the United States; in India the figure was in that year 2 per cent (Stewart, 1974, 27). Thirty per cent of the labour force in the Soviet Union is engaged in the agricultural sector, seven times as many as in the United States; the consumption of wheat is roughly the same in both countries, but in 1975 America exported 80 million tons and Russia imported 25 million tons. An American worker needs to save four months' wages to buy a car; a Soviet worker forty-three months'. More disturbing, certainly from the latter's point of view, is that he needs to work 10 hours for the price of a one-litre bottle of vodka, as against the 1.6 hours in the case of the American worker ('The Economist', 18 October 1975 and 31 January 1976).

COMPARATIVES

Considerable differences were also found between countries within the same industrial sphere.

If the labour productivity in 1955 is set at 100 in Britain, the corresponding figure in West Germany at the same time is 162, in France 167 and in the Netherlands 196. And if the increase in labour productivity between 1955 and 1974 is set at 100 in Britain, the corresponding figure in West Germany is 186, in France 180 and in the Netherlands 248 (Jones, 1976). Here differences in the scope and intensity of investment manifest themselves. But discrepancies arise even where this does not apply. The British Central Policy Review Staff, a 'think tank' which has been commissioned by the government to conduct independent investigations, has concerned itself with the car industry, which certainly is beset with many problems.

Ford manufactured Escorts in a plant in Halewood near Liverpool and in Saarlouis in West Germany. The cars differed only in the position of the steering wheel: right in England, left in Germany. Both plants were built in the 1960s and were identically equipped. Only in Saarlouis 7,165 were employed and in Halewood 10,476, that is, two German workers for every three English workers. In Saarlouis it took 18.5 hours to build a car, in Halewood 44.7 hours.

In Dagenham, near London, Ford also had a plant which made doors for the Cortina; an identical installation was operated in Genk in Belgium. The doors were first stamped and then conveyed along five successive, automatic welding machines. The work consisted primarily of taking the door off the line, placing it in the welding machine and putting the machine into operation by pushing a button. When the operation was completed the door was put back on the assembly line. Apart from this work, which could be learned with some training, a number of mechanics were responsible for maintaining the machines.

In this way 240 doors were produced per hour in Genk and 110 in Dagenham. The study showed that the difference was largely attributable to the mechanics: the ones in the Belgian plant checked and adjusted the machines at regular intervals, while the ones in Dagenham waited in a separate room until something went wrong. The foreman then rang a bell, but it was customary not to react to this; the mechanics started their repair work only after they had been approached in person by the foreman. The machines went wrong quite often and the production line was idle 40 per cent of the time. Once a repair job was completed the mechanics retreated to their room, but the machine operators would only resume work when the foreman became insistent, and this meant further delays. The report emphasizes the monotony of assembly-line work and thus touches upon a factor which is being discussed more and more often in the literature, a fact which rather blunts Schumacher's complaint that the question of 'what the worker does to the worker?' is largely dealt with only in passing (Schumacher, 1975, 18).

The topic is, however, treated exhaustively in the marxist tradition, and the renewed interest in this school has focused attention on it once more. Here the Protestant ethic which saw labour as a source of worldly satisfaction converges with the marxist and existentialist perception of work as an act of self-realization - a convergence which may explain the vehemence with which the younger generation rejects factory labour, which is neither liberating nor creative, but dulling, exhausting and exploitative. It is rather odd that Thoreau has been forgotten, for he preached self-sufficiency before everybody else did. Thoreau rejected all labour except for the *agricola laboriosus* necessary to cultivate one's plot of land. 'Abstain from action', he counselled, for in work man is fleeing from himself; introspection is the fruit of idleness. Here the philosopher touches upon what Diggins calls 'the terrible secret that work may be a neurotic activity intended to divert the mind from the diminution of time and the approach of death' (1972, 585).

In American and European studies of the appreciation of work, the following emerged: the daily task may have become easier, and the working day shorter, but the aversion is undeniable, except that the dislike lessens as the rewards increase (Scitovsky, 1976, 96). This finding can be conveniently linked to the neither philosophically nor psychologically carefully thought-out view that applies in economic theory, which sees labour as the sacrifice made in return for an income. This leads one back to the picture of the carrot being dangled before the unwilling donkey in order to persuade it to continue in the desired direction. It is therefore hardly surprising that when confronted with low labour productivity in their industry, the workers in the English car factory retort that 'you get the labour you pay for'. They of course know that the Belgian and German workers earn considerably more, although this is justified precisely by their higher productivity.

Considering that within the Western cultural sphere there are so many differing views on the role of labour and work and such discrepancies in job performance, it is to be expected that outside this culture and in an early-industrial situation greater rather than smaller deviations will be encountered. Berger et al. point out that in a society where economic activities are restricted to agriculture, work is performed in different rhythms and has a different meaning for those who engage in it.

'The problem of modernization', they write, 'is not to get people to work, but to get them to work in a particular way' (1974, 112). Besides reports of reluctance and resistance, absenteeism and industrial sabotage, there are reports of peasants who work indefatigably under the tropical sun.

At issue is the question whether the economic prescription for obtaining satisfactory performance, that is by offering higher compensation, is universally effective.

13 Tarnished inheritance

'When the multipliers calculated from the model are ranked in order of importance, the majority of the ones above the median are non-economic in nature.' (Adelman)

Only after the Second World War and the decolonization that followed did economic theory turn its attention to the problems of the - predominantly tropical - countries whose economic system had until then been regarded primarily as an extension of the activities of the mother country; an interpretation which, some say, still holds for present conditions. Where the new political entities were elevated to the status of distinct field of study, the economist brought to bear the whole scientific apparatus which had been developed within the European-American intellectual sphere and of late was under the spell of the Keynesian paradigm. As the master himself wrote: 'We take as given the existing skill and quantity of available labour, the existing quality and quantity of available equipment, the existing techniques, the degree of competition, the tastes and habits of the consumer, the disutility of different intensities of labour and of the activities of supervision and organization, as well as the social structure. This does not mean that we assume these factors to be constant; but merely that, in this place and context, we are not considering or taking into account the effects and consequences of changes in them' (Keynes, 1936, 245).

Accordingly, most of the theoretical work on economic growth since the 1950s has kept aloof from what are after all important determinants of wealth. Capital coefficients, shadow prices and so on are instruments generally applied in development planning, they are susceptible of mathematical presentation and model-building; but the human behaviour that lies behind them and which evokes the documented phenomena is not explained by these concepts nor is it influenced by the development plan. As late as 1962 Kaldor could still write: 'It is the limitation of resources, and *not* adequate incentives, which limits the pace of economic development' (1965, 170). The approach which follows from this attitude is reminiscent of the so-called crash programme which is occasionally resorted to in the United States in order to complete a major project, by concentrating all available resources on, say, developing an atom bomb or putting a man on the moon. The development of a poor country is brought about by providing capital on a massive scale; the 'big push' in the right direction will conclusively resolve the problem. But in as recent a work as that of Schiavo-Campo, written after many large-scale investments had proved ineffectual and countless development plans had not got much beyond the archives of the development ministries, there is, after the obligatory recital of the desirability of more capital, more labour and more natural resources, an additional chapter which deals with social dimensions and refers to the 'intangible or residual factor', which turns out to consist of two components: social factors and technology (1970, 69).

THE HAND OF GOD

Cooper deplores the fact that economics has for such a long time looked upon the level and advance of technology as manna from heaven (1975, 295).

True, writers like Sen and Boon refer to technology in explicit terms, but they restrict themselves to an economic-rational choice from an existing set of factor combinations, and appear to have little concern for either the origin or the effect of their application. The American journal 'Technology and Culture', which is dedicated to the history of technology, is, in contrast, always full of pleas for a social-scientific approach to the phenomenon of technology. The historical perspective ought not only to highlight 'how things are done and made' but also 'why things are done and made as they are; what effects have these ... upon those areas of human activity (and) how have other elements in society and culture affected (technology)' (Rürup, 1974, 182). This broad approach is absent in development economics, even in the treatises on adapted technology offered by the Intermediate Technology Group of the World Bank, which in fact still advocates injections of capital, though in different machines and on a different scale.

Forbes, a historian of technology, treats the subject

as a coherent system rather than as a set of distinct machines and techniques. In ancient times, before the agricultural states (initially in the Middle East), began to develop into urban communities, technology exhausted itself in the adaptation of resources to the natural environment. Forbes locates the cause for the differentiation of cultures here. A similar contention has at times been defended in economics, namely when economic life was presented as primarily determined by geographic and climatic conditions. But once agricultural production begins to yield surpluses, the possibility of urbanization arises, and that will entail exchange, the formation of markets and the specialization of occupations. Mining and the pottery industry, plied in regions less suited to agriculture, may well have constituted an initial division of labour, with miners and potters offering their goods in exchange for the scarce food (Forbes, 1968, 8).

Apart from speculations on the origins of technology, Forbes's book discusses an instinct which is allegedly unique to man and drives him to change and improve the conditions of his existence. Again a similar notion is represented in economic theory, namely in the work of Adam Smith or, much later, Veblen, who also talk of instincts which spur man on to economic action. Both authors attribute the advance of rationality to this drive. The need to make choices and the awareness that one choice excludes another (so that the excluded option becomes the sacrifice made for the realization of the chosen option) has allegedly fostered cost consciousness and invested thought with a degree of linearity. The case was put most trenchantly by Schumpeter, who speaks of a 'social process which rationalizes our life and thought' and summarizes it succinctly: 'The economic pattern is the matrix of logic' (1944, 123). Historians of the Enlightenment are similarly inclined to detect a technological and economic element in the movement. 'The Enlightenment prepared men's minds to test every social activity according to the norm of efficiency' (Shriver, 1972, 536). A mind motivated by technology 'idolizes the single value of efficiency, it searches unceasingly for the one best way to do the work.' The spread of this mentality then becomes a matter of cultural diffusion: at a certain juncture it originated in the countries which subsequently rose to ever greater power and wealth and which industrialized to a point where they are now described as post-industrial. Outside of this cultural sphere a number of more or less successful attempts at emulation were undertaken. But within the industrial countries technology was developed by the very people who used it in their daily lives. To the extent that conflicts with other cultural elements arose, they developed slowly and there was ample opportunity to adapt. Not that adaptation was always complete or easy: the 'lags' to which Ogburn referred indicate a degree of dislocation in a culture in which technical development seemed to advance faster than the capacity for absorption would allow. And the sense of crisis which a writer like Ellul links to technology is indicative of the fact that the disruption which technical change causes in an already wholly technicized society has not diminished in the course of time. It is hardly surprising, then, that the same technology causes immensely more serious problems of adaptation when it is transferred to a society which is so unprepared to deal with it.

But what is surprising is that the theory of economic development has paid such scant attention to this problem. Where there is an awareness of the problem it is coupled to the assumption, sometimes implicit, sometimes explicit, that radical social change as a result of the industrial growth of the undeveloped country is unavoidable. When implicit, the assumption is at the root of the development plans which posit the goal of a modern and prosperous society whose elements are derived from the European-American industrial pattern. The existing traditional society is marked as the starting point and the plans will show how a thrust from one to the other can be achieved. Thus in his famous theory of economic take-off, Rostow describes the 'traditional society' as stagnating, defeatist, apathetic; it is characterized by the pre-Newtonian mentality and the constant production function. The aim of a strategy of advance is the 'age of high mass consumption', with the United States as an object lesson.

Initially Rostow intended only historiography: this is how it happened, in this way the wealthy countries advanced from one phase to the next. Later the theory became strategy: so to move one rung up the ladder, for instance, the savings ratio had to be brought up to over 10 per cent. The 'propensity to have children' had to be reduced. Ferkiss goes even further by proclaiming the United States the 'proto-type of the new civilization'. 'In time the world will follow the model of man as made in the U.S.' (1973). So too Drucker: 'Every single one of the new countries ... sees its goal in its transformation into a Western state, economy and society' (1973, 138).

Other writers follow Rostow in cataloguing the necessary modern traits: the poor man in the poor country must develop 'a tinkering attitude', he must be ready to do puzzles, because problems are there to be solved; he must become habituated to anonymous social relations, to rational ('post-Newtonian') thought, to the application of the maximization principle (Berger et al., 1974). If the attempted social reforms cause a dislocation of the indigenous culture, it should be borne in mind, according to Slotkin, that this is a necessary condition for industrial development (1960).

As an explanation of this apparently unanimous desire of the whole of the non-West to imitate the West at all cost, Van Baal notes that the Western view of life is invariably the predominant one in the relations between cultures. The Indonesian anthropologist Koentjaraningrat denies this: the Indonesians, for instance, would be willing to adopt those elements of Western culture which will promote development (1975, 179). For this goal certain elements of Javanese culture would indeed be jettisoned: submissiveness to superiors, unwillingness to accept responsibility, strong orientation to the community, pessimism, mysticism. Other writers tend towards a pragmatic standpoint: the influence of the West is already so great, many developing countries are already so westernized, that it is only sensible to join in.

Berger et al. call 'westernization' a social fact which is also reflected in the subjective perceptions of the population in the countries concerned (1974, 119). Mazrui considers the intensive activities of missionaries and mission schools to be a main cause of this phenomenon. Non-Christian Africans have over the generations also been subjected to their influence and have adapted their values to it to a greater or lesser extent. 'Many in Africa have acquired scruples that neither they nor their parents thought of in the past' (1975, 466).

THE HARD HAND

The idea that now, after the inculcation of the Christian values, it is the West's mission to pass on all its other values is strongly supported by Myrdal, who devotes part of his 'Asian Drama' to it. This Nobel Prize-winner would like to see the following characteristics eliminated:

> Low levels of work discipline, of punctuality and orderliness, superstitious beliefs and irrational outlook; lack of alertness, adaptability, ambition, and general readiness for change and experiment; contempt for manual work, submissiveness to authority and exploitation; low aptitude for cooperation, low standards of personal hygiene and so on' (1968, 1909-10).

In the countries of Southeast Asia it is necessary, Myrdal

argues, radically to reform by force, if need be, the whole gamut of human behaviour, attitudes and institutions. Differences of culture, language and ethnicity which mar the region are to be removed. In turn, social discipline in particular will have to be stepped up. This is the way to obtain economic development.

Measures to counter socially undesirable phenomena should not be delayed. Traditionally there is a feeling that, in so far as it is necessary, change will come about in the long run. During the phase of decolonization many an opponent of the transfer of sovereignty warned that 'they're not yet ready for self-government - it may take centuries'. It may be assumed that even this circle would accept that a few centuries of training would make some kind of impact. But Myrdal urges haste; he deplores the 'gradualist approach' which he imputes to the Asians: 'The bigger and more rapid change ... must be attained by resolutely altering the institutions within which people live and work' (1968, 116).

The idea that a sudden break, or at least a strongly accelerated development is preferable to a slow adaptation stretching over generations gains the approval of Mead. She relies here on her experiences with the Manus, whom she studied twice with a twenty-five year interval, during which time contact with the West effected surprising changes in the culture. She pleads for as complete an adoption of Western institutions as is possible.

> The Manus experience (suggests) that rapid change is not only possible, but may actually be very desirable, that instead of advocating partial change we should advocate that a people, who choose to practise a new technology or enter into drastically new kinds of economic relationships will do this more easily if they live in different houses, wear different clothes, and eat different, or differently cooked, food (1956).

She feels that well-meaning Westerners have for too long resorted to holistic arguments to justify the preservation of indigenous institutions, and that they have for too long encouraged only the adoption of a few selected Western achievements which were thought valuable, such as the Christian values, a bit of literacy (though there was nothing to read) and a bit of arithmetic (though there was nothing to add up). But the Manus have forcefully taken the task of modernization in hand. 'They redesigned their culture from top to bottom.' Yet during her second visit Mead found no evidence of alienation, disorientation or loneliness. She wonders whether more general conclusions might be drawn from the fate of this one people. In some respects a culture is like a language: both show internal coherence of the elements and in both cases one can learn a second one. In both cases one jumps from one pattern to another. 'Then it is important that they should change from one whole pattern to another, not merely patch and botch the old way of life with corrugated iron and discarded tin cans' (Mead, 1956). In 1970 she had not changed her mind: the necessary changes must be implemented within the time span of one generation. Now she is arguing for a new theory of rapid social change which comprises both the transferring and the receiving culture and in this way helps to clarify development problems (1970, 51).

Those economists who propose, largely in ignorance of the anthropological implications, a shock therapy, are firmly within the capitalist camp. But the preference for a sharp break with tradition they share with their radical colleagues, who are also convinced of the need for profound social change, except that they have in mind the emulation of the Chinese or Cuban model. 'Given transformation along the lines of the Chinese revolution, correct technology will follow automatically' (Stewart, 1974, 32).

Here too considerable stress is put on the hard-handed approach: elimination of the elite, the exploiting upper layer, coercion to perform allegedly socially necessary labour, re-education of minds so that all will rejoice in the new ways. In a slightly toned-down version these ideas are also found in the somewhat less radical Stewart, who, as shown earlier, has a certain conception of 'basic needs' and wants to bring production in line with them and thereby change 'the system' as a whole. Marginal change, she believes, will not achieve these objectives (1974, 25).

Anyone who is reasonably well read in the social sciences, or is perhaps just superficially aware of the programmes of progressive politicians, knows that there is change, that there will need to be more change, and that this means above all an alteration of 'the structures'. Social changes occur through time; that which arrives on the scene later is more modern, though still only contemporary; that which will arrive even later lies in the future, which - if all goes as envisaged by the progressive planner - will be even better because it will be really 'modern'. 'Modern man' is one to whom are ascribed positive qualities. It may be the institutions that have been 're-institutionalized', the values which have been re-valued, but in the end what matters is man himself: faith, value, institution, even structure, are only abstractions that are appealing to the ear but really only exist in a manner of speaking.

So people will have to change in order to become modern, and because speed is always of the essence in the implementation of socio-cultural reform plans, this must not take generations. But does man lend himself so readily to undergoing changes in his life, and particularly in his later life? There is a school of psychology which believes not; 'We are pessimistic about producing major changes in a (personal) characteristic after it has reached a level of stability' (Bloom, 1964, 218). Sociologists, too, while happily describing and promoting social change, often believe that a number of basic traits of the individual, corresponding to his cultural (sub-) pattern of which he is a part by accident of birth, are formed in what is now called early socialization. This base is relatively constant. Like the psychologists, they assume that the flexibility which is a precondition for the reformation of the basic personality declines with age.

An economist who has ventured into this field, namely Hagen, thus came to the conclusion that the other, modern mentality which should be the precondition for any economic development can only be brought about by profoundly rethinking the education of young children.

This view suggests that through succeeding experiences to which the individual is exposed, by education or otherwise, there emerge 'layers' of the personality. The image is reminiscent of the annual rings of a tree and it has the same historical implications: that which came earlier is located lower down, deeper. Spiro once invoked a remarkable analogy with an onion: the deepest leaves which were the first to grow are best protected.

Anthropological studies have shown that what is learned at an early age will indeed stick (Leis, 1964, 32). A functionalist explanation can be supplied for the devotee by assuming that *those* traits which are perceived as the ones most closely connected to certain others are the ones that will be relinquished last. This raises hopes for changes which are required in order to industrialize what was hitherto an agricultural society.

The new behaviour here required is, to use a term coined by Kriesberg, 'serially independent', that is to say, there are few points of contact with deep-seated behaviour patterns: in terms of traditional society a job in industry constitutes a break with the old behaviour pattern. The choice in itself indicates that one is less dominated by the norms learned at an early age. This choice must of course lie within the scope of perceived possibilities; according to Kriesberg this depends on what he calls situational factors, the factual circumstances in which the individual finds himself (1963, 581).

THE GENTLE HAND

Modern is everything that is new, that replaces the existing, has just replaced it or is about to replace it. Development of a country which (compared to developments elsewhere) has remained backward occurs through a renewal of technology. This technology is applied, executed and improved: modernized! The people involved are inculcated with something other than the influences to which they have been subjected in their traditional world. They become modern. As said before, there is in the literature a strong tendency to equate modernization with westernization; but this is rather unhistorical. Every step which, development being its goal, brings an aspired condition nearer, heralds a phase which is modern compared to the previous, though it can still be very different from what is considered modern in the industrial countries. A well in a village where previously the women had to carry water from a river is a useful modernization, but still far removed from hot and cold running water. Charcoal for cooking is modern compared to dried cow dung, but it is still far from a gas cooker, let alone a microwave oven.

'Modern man' is an ideal type, often posited as a counterpart to traditional man. Dichotomies of this kind are favoured by sociologists: with Redfield one is 'folk' or 'urban', with Riesman 'inner-' or 'other-directed' - in these cases the former type fits into an earlier, the latter into a later historical stage. This typology appears in a development perspective in Lerner's well-known 'The Passing of Traditional Society'. It cites a Turkish shopkeeper who, when questioned about his plans for the future, describes the kind of shop he would like to own - it turns out to be a mirror image of the modern self-service store. Inkeles and Smith have found modern man in Pakistan. He has had one year of schooling and has worked for ten years in a metalworks, where he is a moulder. He is only moderately satisfied with his job but prefers it to agricultural work. His wage is high, he can, as he puts it, live well and even send money home at the end of the month. He likes the new life: 'We can meet different people in town' (1974, 74). Against this a peasant showed himself a traditional figure. He wished to be spared any new experiences and considered it an advantage that, unlike factory workers, he could always stay at home. 'I can get crops by the grace of the almighty and can live with my wife, children and parents'. Inkeles and Smith did not leave it at documenting these two cases, and put their interviewers on to 6,000 people in six developing countries in Asia, Africa and Latin America. Peasants, factory workers, civil servants, shopkeepers, all were attacked with questionnaires which were based on a modernity syndrome with twenty-four dimensions. The results are documented in 'Becoming Modern', and this is above all a study of how people's mentality and behaviour are influenced by working in an industrial environment. The starting point is again that the inevitable changes which accompany development presuppose the existence of a certain level of modernity in those affected. It is they who populate the workshops and factories. If they do not adapt to the demands which industrial labour makes on them, development will fail. They will have to have an open mind about the new environment in which they are placed, orient themselves to the future, credit themselves with a certain power to control their environment, esteem technical knowledge and show a willingness to learn new methods. All these characteristics were found in the persons employed in an industrial plant, and they were more strongly developed among those who had been there longer. Apart from the level of education, it was the industrial experience which had exerted the most powerful influence over the individual. 'The factory is a school of modernity' (1974, 273). And 'Technology (is) the most distinctive ingredient of modernity' (314).

In the factory, where technology is most visible and tangible, the individual spends five or six days a week, at least eight hours a day, year in, year out. Most often he has entered it at quite a young age and he will invariably be moulded by such a profound and lengthy work experience. He starts to acquire the characteristics which bring him in line with the criteria of modernity.

Still not satisfied with the confirmation of their hypothesis, Inkeles and Smith subsequently tried to determine which factors in the industrial situation possessed the greatest modernizing value. The new hypothesis was that the most modern plant would also have the most modernized workers in its employment.

Small workshops with few machines and a limited number of employees were supposed to be more closely linked to the traditional sphere, which was precisely the one that was an impediment to development. For this reason only firms with at least fifty employees and an extensive range of energy-intensive machines were chosen. A wholly automated crown cork factory in Nigeria, which supplied the country's breweries and soft drink factories with corks, was not included in the sample because it gave work to only thirty people. A firm in Pakistan with a staff of a thousand was not included because a paternalistic atmosphere was observed and, contrarily, in the production process the safety of the workers was neglected. The researcher apparently considered this a traditional trait.

Later he came back to this, when it turned out that in three of the five countries no correlation could be shown to exist between the degree to which the plant could be classified as modern and the level of modernity observed among the staff. The remark of the researcher who had rejected the Pakistani firm as 'too traditional' is most revealing:

> Many of the workers (in this firm) had to apply higher skills than workers in a much more modern factory. The modern factory will not necessarily be the one where the men actually have more contact with modern techniques. *These men were having contact not with absolutely modern techniques, but with techniques that were modern as compared to what they may have practised in their village.* And they were having more intimate contact with these techniques (Inkeles, 1974, 184).

Inkeles and Smith go on to say that they noticed that the equipment in the most modern factories was removed from sight, its operation was hardly visible and without a doubt incomprehensible to the workmen, no matter how long they had been involved with it: they perfunctorily performed the tasks without any understanding. In the less modernly equipped factory the workers knew precisely what purpose everything served, how it worked, and what could go wrong. 'From the standpoint of a man's actual contact with the industrial process, I am not sure at all that (this factory) is backward as a learning experience' (1974, 185). This is an important observation which lends support to the view that the technology to be introduced in development should be intermediate - here understood to mean offering an optimal chance for the members of the new industrial community to fathom the functions, to grasp their role in the whole and to be able to identify with the work process and aims.

It is a pity that Inkeles and Smith only arrived at these conclusions very late in the course of their investigation. Not so much because the whole effort of observing factories and classifying them as modern or not had an unsatisfactory outcome and disproved the hypothesis. Finding no evidence to corroborate a reasonable supposition also contributes to knowledge.

It would have been much more significant if criteria had been found which were shared by the various factories in the various countries and which did correlate positively with the 'modern' characteristics of the staff. Or, to be less pretentious and less general and perhaps more attuned to what the diversity of culture would lead one to expect, there surely must be significant data in plant structure, management policy, and location (city-countryside) which could explain the higher or lower level of modernity among factory workers.

In the literature on modernization it is urbanization that is often adduced as an explanation. Hoselitz, for instance, sees the cities in the Third World as the 'chief locus for the introduction of new ideas and new ways of doing things'. They are also the 'crucial places in which the adaptation ... of new techniques ... and production patterns is achieved' (1962, 163). The sprawling cities with their impoverished slum populations have meanwhile exposed the seamy side of urbanization. Consequently, where a demographic policy actually exists, it will more likely be aimed at reversing migration to the towns rather than encouraging it for the sake of modernization. Inkeles and Smith found that the level of modernity of city dwellers is related to their involvement in an industrial situation. The 'urban, non-industrial' workers lagged in this respect behind those that worked in a factory, irrespective of how long they had lived in the city.

This too will please the advocates of intermediate technology, which is after all about starting industrial plants in the countryside, which will, it is hoped, narrow differences in income, spread employment and alleviate transport problems.

It is also quite likely that a technology which links up better with traditional methods will meet with at least the same if not a better response in the countryside than in the cities.

Another idea which contemporary Western culture has toyed with is that of the involvement of the employees in the management of their firm. If it is true, as must be suspected on the basis of Inkeles and Smith's findings, that modernization is more effective when employees are in a position to gain a better understanding of the workings of the firm as a whole, then involvement will become stronger if they have a voice in management. Whether local traditions are amenable to this remains to be seen, and one may wonder whether the experiments which are being carried out in the developing countries do not appeal more to those devising them than to those subjected to them. Inkeles and Smith here show themselves somewhat biased. This became apparent just now, when the American observer in the Pakistani factory expressed his surprise at the lack of safety precautions. After many years and many accidents, industrial safety is now so interwoven with

Western management that one cannot imagine machines without guards or workers without helmets. The workers in Pakistan did not even wear shoes. Furthermore, despite all protestations, Inkeles and Smith's modern man continues to look very Western. He is a man of action, aware that he controls his destiny, ambitious, thirsting for knowledge and the acquisition of new skills. And he prefers consuming to saving. One can defend this by arguing that Western man developed as he did by being exposed to the same influences to which the non-Westerner, in his striving for Western-oriented wealth, is now exposed. This leads to the aforementioned convergence of cultures. Several writers have pointed to the penetration of Western dress not only to the cities of the tropical world but also to their most remote rural areas. The ballpoint pen and the wristwatch have become the symbols of modernity; they attest to the literacy of the possessor, and, even more revealing, the watch shows him as a man who knows what time it is.

The clock only came into general use when it was needed, during the industrial revolution. Punctuality is imperative in the factory; in the fields an hour is neither here nor there. The 'terror of hour and fact' lamented in the West in poetic distaste for modern technology is evidently a coveted goal in countries which have until now escaped its vexations, but where those who can afford it are already providing themselves with the trappings.

But the following two passages bring to light another objection to Inkeles and Smith's work: 'We decided our conception of the modern man in part from the form of conduct we saw as likely to be inculcated by work in the factory' (1974, 5); and: 'We decided ... to peg our list of modern qualities more specifically to the particular requirements of running a factory' (18).

Once one has decided to define modernity as the totality of characteristics needed to be successful in a factory environment, then it is hardly surprising that a study among staff which, after selection, is found in the factory will indeed possess those characteristics.

Through the force of mission and media, schooling and ever-present example, Western industrial culture has left a deep impression. For this reason alone Mazrui is tempted to define the relation between the non-West and the West as one of dependence (1975). Small wonder that in these countries there are groups who are only too happy to deny their own totem and aspire to be included in this higher, prominent and moreover prosperous sphere.

If one wanted really to deflate Inkeles and Smith, one

could say that all they have uncovered is that there are non-Westerners who have Western aspirations and that these aspirations are elaborated as rewards increase. This does not alter the fact that the learning process, assuming end and means are acceptable, is essential to development. In a philosophical essay on tools Feibleman writes: 'If learning consists in eliciting from responses the capacity to respond, then man is taught by his response to the stimulation of his tools!' (1967, 333).

HUMAN LABOUR

Economists recognized quite early on that men need time to master a new production process: the familiar 'infant industry argument' for tariff protection of the new industry is based on the idea that there needs to be a starting period in which industry should be allowed to work undisturbed, until enough experience is gathered for it to be able to act independently. For a start it has been shown that the construction of plants proceeds more smoothly if the supplying capital-goods industry has built the installation before. For the chemical industry it is thought that maximum efficiency of construction is reached only after the contractor has built five or six similar plants (Stewart, 1977, 132). Once the installation is put into operation, teething troubles appear: a series of faults holds up production, machines are wrongly adjusted, products are below standard. The following phase is still one of below-optimum productivity. Apart from knowledge codified in manuals and laid down in regulations, a smooth-running production process seems to require a certain insight which is obtained only after some experience with the installation. Here is manifested 'disembodied technical progress', the residual factor to which growth theory invariably takes recourse when a rise in productivity cannot be explained by increased capitalization. Lundberg has studied the phenomenon at a micro-economic level in a Swedish steel plant, where a new but subsequently unchanged production method yielded steadily rising production per man-hour (this being the smallest unit by which economic development can be measured). He offered as an explanation the 'favourable responses' from the participants in the production process. Arrow has analysed this and other material and indicates that a learning process is at work here (1962, 155-73). In a country which lacks the technical substratum on which Lundberg's plant could rely, greater problems may be expected to develop - again all the more reason to follow on from traditional skills when choosing a technique (Selwyn, 1973, 18). But more is expected of the new technical sphere of influence. Rosenberg has hopes not only for new technical skills, but also for changed 'aptitudes' and 'aspirations' (1976, 87). It is true that an industrial enterprise will not remain isolated from its environment and that those who spend a sizeable part of their life in that sphere will show signs of their new mentality outside it. Rosenberg speaks of a recoiling upon society and Inkeles sees it as a continuation of the process of socialization which inaugurates general modernization. '(The) factory experience will be generalized' (Inkeles and Smith, 1974, 159).

Naipaul, an East Indian born in Trinidad who visits India regularly and, as a novelist, has written of India with a sharpness that exceeds that of much social-scientific analysis, visited a slum in Bombay and found there the chaotic, sickening mess of refuse and excrement which are the environment of the Indian shanty town: 'Little dark rooms, often no more than boxes, often with just a bed on the earth floor, ... little black runnels of filth between the rooms, occasional enfeebled rats struggling up the gutters, slimy where steep, scum quickly forming around impediments of garbage' (1977, 67). But one neighbourhood is different: there the streets are clean, paved instead of muddy, there are latrines and wash-houses and even a little square cleared of huts. The organization is in the hands of an engineer who wished to do something to better the lot of the poor and of a mechanic working for Air India. Most of the male population are factory workers. Naipaul concludes from this that 'Industrial workers (here were) beginning to apply something of the discipline of the factory floor to the areas where they lived' (1977, 64).

A sharp mind, untainted by development-sociological designs, here unintentionally supplies an illustration of the mechanisms which are dealt with in the above-mentioned publications.

These mechanisms are not newly discovered: they are at the core of the materialist conception of history, which holds that, as Feibleman succinctly puts it, man is made by his tools: the intellectual climate of society - with all the values, norms, and institutions which a sociologist detects in it - is altered when the material base shifts. And this is brought about by changes in technology, corresponding to Marx's scheme of the society of the windmill passing into the society of the steam engine.

In 1853 Marx deduced from reports by British colonial administrators that the Indian population coped quite well with the demands which factory labour of that time made of them. This does not astonish Marxist sociologists - after all, this manifests merely a specific instance of the general rule. 'Here, too, the technological basis paves the way for changes in production ... new interactions between the means of labour and man ... are taking place' (Drobyshev and Vafa, 1974, 213). However, the knowledge on which the new and constantly renewed production method is based is denied to the industrial workers in the developing countries. They only do the work; as to the what, how and why, that only the designers of the technique really understand, and they are elsewhere, abroad or in an upper crust, removed from the sphere of day-to-day factory work. The techniques remain alien entities; they are grafted upon the community in a way which precludes endogenous growth. To use an analogy: the genetic material which carries the code of Western culture fails to fertilize the recipient culture. The gap was not closed during the colonial phase. This is one of the main components of the enduring dependence. The Sussex Manifesto expresses it as follows:

> The real causes lie ... in the nature of underdevelopment itself ... many of the structural and organizational characteristics of the developing economies are antithetical to the application of science and technology. (This) underlies both the limited transfer of technology into local industries in the developing countries and also the weak development of local scientific institutions (Sussex Manifesto, 1974, 9).

MANUAL LABOUR

All this presumes the undesirability of isolation. There is also a school which champions protecting and preserving local peculiarities. The values which give meaning to life should not be interfered with, let alone purposely re-formed. This standpoint might be understandable when adopted by a conservative anthropologist, who is lamenting the disappearance of his subject matter, whose otherness he cherishes. But the economist Bauer appears to espouse this view when he reproaches Myrdal for harbouring the misconception that people live only for the sake of tangible economic attainment. Bauer enjoins us not to belittle the happiness conferred by a cultural pattern that knows the tranquility of 'mysticism and ... renunciation of the world compared to acquisition and achievement' (1976, 78). This view is shared by Boeke, who pleaded for 'village restoration' already in 1931 and again in

1952: the local population is not well served by all these interventions intent on rapid development, for even if they succeed they only lead to disintegration. As Higgins concludes in a summary of Boeke's theory of dualism: 'The kindest thing the Western world can do for underdeveloped areas is to leave them alone' (1959, 227).

In India these ideas have, despite all development policy, survived. Gandhi consistently fought for the preservation of or the return to simple village life, with the simple spinning wheel as a symbol that acquired even national significance. Manual work carried out in poverty ennobles. Naipaul encountered these feelings throughout India - the poor are fashionable there. A lady from the middle classes spoke with satisfaction about 'The happiness of the poor - greater than the happiness of others' (1977, 137). An old congressman looked upon India's poverty as something very special. 'As a Gandhian, he didn't want to see anyone spoiling it. (He) disliked machines and had heard that people in the West had begun to turn against them as well' (1977, 151). In Indonesia Geertz observed poverty and the unchangeability of patterns of behaviour. To describe it he coined the term 'agricultural involution': as more mouths needed to be fed agricultural labour became more and more intensive, but the method of (manual) work stayed the same. And as returns diminished there was less for each new mouth.

Discussions of the phenomenon of technology invariably include the key terms voluntarism and modernism.

There is talk of Enlightenment and Progress.

The attitude is undeniably Western and the transfer of the material results of this culture - machines, industry - means an adaptation on the part of the recipient culture which amounts to a radical reformation.

This has always been recognized in the discussion on technology transfer. Differences of opinion have arisen mainly with regard to the speed at which the re-culturation is to proceed: the gradualists (among whom are also some economists) oppose the shock therapists (among whom are also some anthropologists). Adaptation of technology appears in the contemporary phase of the debate as a pragmatic intermediate standpoint: the question as to the how prevails over the how fast.

Systematic observation of development-industrial success or failure must provide insights into how socio-cultural force is lent to technical adaptation.

14 Corruptible progress

> 'Was life in traditional society so satisfactory that its transformation was an act of criminal negligence?' (Kindleberger)

Western, or Western-derived, reflection focuses with some regularity on the categories *homo ludens* and *homo faber*, playing man and working man, where the former activity is also thought to have economic utility. For Veblen, play expresses man's 'idle curiosity'. True, man investigates nature to satisfy his curiosity, but his ulterior motive is to put to use whatever he finds, to gain from his discovery in some way. There probably were times when the interest was a purely detached one. This might have been so in classical Athens; but then Bowra believes that this explains at least in part the decline of that civilization, since slave labour freed the citizen from all drudgery and the application of knowledge was considered undignified (1971, 81). Sombart located the acceleration of the industrial revolution in eighteenth-century England, where after widespread deforestation the shortage of wood led to the mining of coal, a source of energy which in turn sparked off the spectacular growth of the iron industry. In due course technical innovations began to succeed each other rapidly. 'The age', said Dr Johnson, who is often quoted in this context, 'is running mad after innovation.' Since the age of classical economics, economists have frequently availed themselves of the concept of innovation: Ricardo to explain the initial advantage that accrued to the first person to apply an invention, Schumpeter to explain development and the business cycle. A new production method may result in a fall in price, use less raw materials, or less labour, bring forth a new product or improve an existing one - all these factors provide a stimulus to economic life. Discovery for its own sake, called research and development, has become a pursuit in its own right in the industrial countries. In German the shift is expressed with some subtlety: *finden*, to chance upon, has become *erfinden*, to invent.

Firms build laboratories and take on staff purely to accelerate technical development, hoping to gain an advantage over their competitors, who engage in equally frenzied activity to keep up. The state offers financial support, pure research is encouraged in the hope of 'spin-offs'. Machlup has calculated that the 'knowledge-producing occupations' have trebled between 1900 and 1960 (1962, 396). Expenditure on research has in most Western countries risen faster than the national income. The amount spent in this field is often taken as an indicator of the prospective increase in wealth. One cannot really quarrel with Whitehead's judgment in his famous 'Science and the Modern World': 'The greatest invention has been the invention of the method of invention.' (1925). This cultural attainment has been limited primarily to the countries of Europe and North America and - of late - Japan. It is possible that other cultures will develop along different lines and that there this particular quality will be absent or stunted. Thus Nash introduces his description of the economy of Mexican Indians as follows:

> I hope to show how the structure and membership criteria of production units limit maximization; how the level and rhythm of output are consequences of the ceremonial cycle and how notions of witchcraft and the supernatural combine to keep wealth from being used for economic ends and thus contribute to the steady state of small reduplicative, productive units with little interest in, or incentive for, technological or social innovation (1961, 186).

Another view is articulated by the *dependencia* school, which believes that the striving for technical innovation, where present, is nipped in the bud by the competition of Western techniques imported into the developing country. It is not always clear to what extent the descriptions reflect reality and to what extent they embody the personal views of the observer.

SOURED CIVILIZATION

Earlier the question was raised as to how far the 'traditional culture' recorded in the literature or even in the consciousness of the observer actually accords with reality: Ranger mentions well-meaning Europeans who fabricated cultural traits which were subsequently championed by the local elite and so created the myth of an idyllic, egalitarian society in the pre-colonial past, of 'négritude', harking back to a past that never was. Naipaul observes the same phenomenon: 'Even the ideas Indians have of the achievements of their civilization are essentially the ideas given by European scholars in the nineteenth century' (1977, 124).

He doubts whether the Europeans, heavily burdened with cultural preconceptions of their own, could ever comprehend Indian reality: 'They missed too much.' He recalls that Gandhi, a fertile source of ideas on traditional India that is now tapped again by the advocates of intermediate technology, was inspired by Tolstoy; how he decided 'he was a Hindu' during his student days in London; and how he formed his ideas on the relationship between races during his stay in South Africa. The wounds inflicted on India which Naipaul describes in his 'Wounded Civilization' stem from the clinging to historical fictions: 'The civilization they have inherited has long gone sour' (1977, 109).

Western civilization, on the other hand, though more successful in the creation of (material) wealth, has throughout retained an (intellectual) current which deplores the attendant phenomena or even wealth itself: in America the outsider Thoreau, whose 'Walden' is as popular as ever, so that the local tourist office reports an increasing number of visitors to his pond; in France Rousseau and his innocent and happy savages, with high prices being paid for the naive works of art by his customs-officer namesake; in Britain Morris, equally hankering after nature; but of course above all in Germany, with its romantics abandoning themselves to 'Weltschmerz', predicting the decline of the West or believing it was already happening - their line runs through to Fromm and Marcuse. Civilization apparently has its fair share of 'discontents', everyday life has its fair share of psychopathology. The philosophical current of existentialism, widespread in the 1950s, saw human feelings of inadequacy as inherent in the 'human condition': the awareness of finiteness and mortality inevitably permeated consciousness. It is perhaps the rise of sociology which has served to dispel these representations of man as a loner, to put above all social man in his place. Inadequacy is now no longer perceived as caused by external factors: the community is too socialized, too atomized, too rationalized, too depressing or even repressive. Since not only human life but also the number of perceptions of that life are finite, the old images tend to recur. The urban youth of today tends, as did Blake, to see factories as satanic inventions. In the comfort of his centrally heated home, the Western intellectual writes about (greater) human dignity in a (poorer) pre-industrial past and about the desirability of bringing industrial development to an immediate halt, shielding mother earth from the technocrats, promoting zero-growth. Mannheim's 'functional rationality', with which economic theory is infatuated, is repudiated as cold and impersonal. In the technical work environment man becomes alienated from himself and he becomes the manipulator of his fellow man. We must go back to the open encounter, to warm (fellow) feeling; those who no longer have any feeling can take a crash course in sensitivity training - the institutionalization of de-institutionalization. And if even that fails there is always the Way of Zen.

Development economists who for years devoted themselves to the cause of rapid industrialization, repented. Singer in his old age reports an 'increasing awareness of the disruptive effects of technology' (1977, 39). Hard technology, where the vestiges of humanity left the worker are numbed by loud music over the PA system, must be replaced with soft technology, inviting a communal song. Until recently the poor countries were exhorted to follow the Western example of industrialization; now this is seen as 'Le Scandale du développement' (Austruy, 1968).

And, not inconsistently, Allahwerdi suggests that the industrial countries must begin by changing themselves (1974, 267). Some look for new social forms outside of America and Europe, and here too the models change with the generations: the Webbs did not doubt for one moment that Russia pointed the way, but when a Soviet official proclaims on American television that 'Our aim is the full automobilization of Soviet society' it is understandable that former admirers of the Soviet experiment have changed their allegiance to China, especially now that Cuba raises doubts and Chile has failed (Berger, 1974, 145).

IMAGINED CIVILIZATION

Earlier the resentment felt by the poor countries at this change of attitude was mentioned. Now that the enthusiasm of the 'development decades' has waned, and the industrial countries have to pay dearly for their oil and spend more on unemployment benefits, the West has suddenly decided that material wealth is no longer desirable and the manner in which that wealth was attained is harmful.

One could point out that zero-growth occurs only where governments are unable to prevent economic stagnation; that the consumption of energy, that very scarce factor, is still rising; and that full automobilization, this noble Soviet ideal, is still relentlessly pursued in the industrial countries despite all the cars. But the idea of simplicity above all else has, as Naipaul observed in India, also gained currency in the poor countries; partly because it has blown over from Europe, 'Backed up by frustrations ... from Western sources', partly out of frustration with the relative failure of economic development which had been hoped for after independence; and finally owing to a rediscovery of historical roots, 'a sinking back into the past, the rediscovery of old ways, "simplicity"!' (1977, 142). An enchanted author quoted earlier remarks that the peasants in Thailand, in accordance with their Buddhist convictions, work to be happy, not to acquire worldly goods. 'The Thai view of life is something to be enjoyed here and now' (Ayal, 1963, 46).

Latter-day hippies and alternative thinkers will be able to identify with this sentiment. Berger et al. note the affinity, which, they feel, is also expressed in the dress of European and American youth. 'Imagined peasant tastes (are) approximated in clothing' and recall the shepherd dances which Marie Antoinette performed with her aristocratic clique at Versailles (1974, 179). The yearning is perhaps the same, the fallacy of abstracting idylls of 'self-sufficiency' from grinding rural poverty most certainly is. Berger et al.'s explanation of this youth culture evokes the Dutch psychologist Van den Berg's existential exposition of the origins of puberty, a phase of life which he suggests was 'invented' at about the same time as the steam engine: the improved survival chances of children made it unnecessary for parents to remain as aloof from them as before. In past times, as infant mortality decimated offspring, the sense of possible, even probable, loss was ever present: '(The) expression of love was inhibited by the realization that the loved child was unlikely to survive' (Berger et al., 1974, 173). Now that death no longer does us part so early and in fact the anxiety for bare survival has practically disappeared in the industrial countries, the parents cherish their smaller 'planned' families so fondly that Berger is moved to speak of 'soft socialization'. The period of infancy and puberty, of carefree youth, is extended, there emerges a 'voluntary association of ex-youths heroically refusing to admit their age'.

The long-deferred confrontation with the harsh demands of a cold society becomes more and more difficult, and the escape into soft alternativism is finally the outcome. Not that 'doing your own thing' indicates individualism; attitudes and dress reveal a strong uniformity - youngsters travelling through the Third World can be detected from afar by their hairstyle and the obligatory faded blue. Naipaul saw them in India, where growing numbers of sitar-playing devotees followed their gurus, occasionally cashing their traveller's cheques from home. For the relaxation and idleness of those who reject industrialism can be pursued only by the grace of those who accept it. A study of attitudes to technology showed that a majority still regards it as beneficial rather than harmful: 'Machines, computers (are seen) as bringing comfort, awareness, efficiency and a high standard of living' (Taviss, 1972, 620). Were this majority to dwindle, the economic dependence of the peripheral groups would be painfully exposed. After all, the market for organically grown produce or artistic basketwork is located in the reviled urbanized centre, whence medical aid and social benefits also derive. The counter-culture is peripheral in the, for its members, disappointing sense that the sustaining culture indeed fulfils the central role. The Western hippies in India are dependent on the non-hippies who have stayed behind in their country of origin: '... the trains running, the presses printing, the rupees arriving from somewhere' (Naipaul, 1977, 25).

The uniform of contemporary Western youth represents a weak attempt to express outwardly the resemblance to the simple peasant, who is found only in the poor countries. But the correspondence goes further: it extends to certain convictions which Foster has described for the peasant community but which, as we shall see, are part of more general human conceptions. This concerns the notion referred to earlier that there is only a limited quantity of the good and desirable and that if one person gets more, another will receive correspondingly less. Foster called this the 'Image of the Limited Good'; he invokes it to explain the disinclination to compete: for as one gains, the other loses. This is demonstrably the case when there is a scarcity of good agricultural land available to a community: when one particular peasant cultivates a larger portion, the others will have less at their disposal. A similar mechanism has also been noted with regard to ideal values. Honour is the reward for courage shown in war, but not every soldier commands homage - it will be accorded a single person or at most a chosen few. When everyone is equally courageous the distinction conferred will be lost.

Some forms of prestige are not divisible at all: there is only one king, only one captain of the ship. Economics has traditionally concerned itself with the value and utility of goods; now the presumption is being made that in an industrial society the social significance of a good in fact surpasses its functional significance. That is to say, as consuming becomes increasingly observable to the community, the function of status symbols tends to predominate. The motor car is not so much a utilitarian means of transport as, through design and price, a means to the consolidation of the status which the owner holds or at least aspires to. Part exchange, as was suggested earlier, offers an opportunity subtly to symbolize in one's means of transport every successive rung on the ladder of social stratification. This understanding of the status function is by now common coin. Less widespread perhaps is the idea, suggested by Riesman already over a generation ago, that the 'Limited Good' analysis applies here: for as the number of consumers who can afford a certain status good grows, the prestige conferred by its possession diminishes. In 'The Lonely Crowd' Riesman referred to the children of well-to-do parents who rejected what their parents were still praising as the delights of sophisticated consumption. In what has in the meantime been dubbed post-industrial society this rejection has been echoed by a wider, though still predominantly younger circle.

REVILED TECHNOLOGY

Bol observes indignantly that in their admiration for the great entrepreneurs - and the greatest are, by virtue of the definition, the multinationals - economists have forgotten that 'one person's gain may be another's loss' (1976, 508). But economics has been imbued with this idea from the beginning: not only the school which explains inequality of income by exploitation, but the mercantilist school - far from averse to capital - also selected the finiteness of resources as the starting point and bluntly argued for an economic policy which would bring in as much as possible for one's own country. The deadly diagnosis, made at the time by Malthus, is generally known, as is the reason why it proved wrong, namely the ability of expanding technical capacity to overcome time and again the constraints of scarcity. It is not difficult to uncover Malthusian elements in the zero-growth argument as first articulated by Meadows and others in 'Limits to Growth' and now widely adhered to. This applies especially to the supposition that technology will not develop further, discussed in greater detail elsewhere (Duller, 1976). Schumacher ventures into a related field when he distinguishes between an economy 'using up reserves' and one 'living off the interest'. The latter idea can be traced back to the classics of economic thought, and for this reason classical economic theory is not very instructive on the subject of a dynamic industrial economy. Despite all the diversity of opinion among economists, there is at least a consensus that it is above all technical progress that has brought the rich countries the wealth which is now so controversial. Those who ignore this, or who recognize it but wish to put a stop to it, fail to appreciate an essential feature of Western society. They are easily seduced into making daft and utterly unsubstantiated statements like 'technology will always cost money', or 'costs of technology are always greater than its benefits' (Clarke, 1973, 262). As far as intermediate technology is concerned, there is a distinct danger that researchers will, instead of pursuing a close alignment with industry (as rightly urged by Stewart) turn away from it and lose themselves in unworldly experiments.

Spending many years wandering around the countryside, like Bhave, a latter-day follower of Gandhi, with the aim of achieving through meditation and prayer a better distribution of land, thus combating poverty, will not, for instance, improve the lot of the poor. 'This walk is just a walk,' says Naipaul, 'none of these villagers may either be giving or getting land' (1977, 164). Bhave moved among villagers in an Indian tradition (Gandhi also walked, though not as far), but Schumacher, father of intermediate technology, equally builds on a tradition: his 'Small is Beautiful' evinces traces; the later 'Guide for the Perplexed' is steeped in it (1977). The 'Four great levels of Being' consist of 'Four elements: matter, life, consciousness and awareness'. 'Man can be written: M; animal can be written M-Z; plants can be written M-Z-Y; mineral can be written M-Z-Y-X' (28; it can be done with plus signs too, see 27). 'The Four Levels of Being are thus seen as pointing to the invisible existence of a Level (or Levels) of Being above the human' (38). 'The Universe is what it is' (46).

And on the next page we indeed encounter the astral body and further on Ouspensky is cited, followed by the Buddhist monk Nyanaponika Thera, who speaks of the 'Ancient Way of Mindfulness' (81). At the National Institute of Design in India Naipaul saw young researchers working on adapted-technological tools in which they had clearly embodied their own romantic ideals rather than considering the needs of the peasant. There was a harvesting machine which to Naipaul seemed a few centuries behind that used by the Romans. It required the peasant to stand up - in India, however, he tends to squat during this work. When this was pointed out to the inventor, he replied that the people would have to be re-educated. 'He had spent a week in the countryside and the peasants had been interested' (1977, 122). Then there were the harvesting shoes with sharp knives attached; the peasant had to execute certain steps amid the crop - a risky harvest dance. Another designer was planning ahead working on a wheelchair. Naipaul considers the institute 'a playpen ... a finishing school for the unacademic young' (123).

A modernizer like Inkeles is very much partial to a voluntarist view of life. He believes that by intervening in the social process a turn-around for the good can be brought about, that by careful analysis human motivations can be discerned and subsequently the accumulated knowledge can be applied to achieve the desired goal. Here he is in the company of the majority of development economists, while many sociologists also seem to think that intervention of this kind is both practicable and desirable. The conceptions of being and wellbeing in traditional culture are often described as belonging to the determinist category: if a development process is taking place, then it is regarded as immanent, as occuring independently of the will and power of human beings. Development economists shake their heads and make accusations of defeatism. The camp which is critical of the results obtained by modernization does not like to put its trust in the immanent course of development either: the notion that the members of a community are free to choose how they organize their society is highly voluntarist and contemporary.

The ideas of Illich mentioned earlier are hence not anti-technological: a Convivial Society could flourish thanks to an advanced, even wholly automated technology which will release large groups of people from monotonous labour and widen the scope for conviviality. This possibility has at times been hinted at for the industrial countries, and some people have wondered anxiously who, with soft socialization continuing, will be left to perform the remaining industrial tasks. Even the air passenger who is totally unconstrained by the Protestant ethic would like to see his aeroplane flown by attentive young people who regularly pay a visit to the hairdresser; and even the most committed prophet of consciousness-expanding drugs would, if he needs medical help, prefer to be operated on by a tee-totaller. It is unsociological to propose not to modernize the developing countries along the difficult path outlined by Inkeles, but instead to let the necessary production processes be carried out as highly automated as the latest chips allow.

As a bit of economic lateral thinking one can envisage a means of distributing the flow of goods over a population other than by the formation of income which presupposes participation in the production process. A system of distribution like the one introduced in the industrial countries in time of war can secure for families a proper share in the national income and offers an ideal opportunity to the supporters of income equality. It will be slightly more difficult to finance the investments, let alone get a return on them. Profit or loss may not be that central in a social organization of this type, but if the funds - which will undoubtedly have to flow in massive quantities and must also guarantee the salaries of foreign experts - will have to come out of the development-aid budgets in the forseeable future, then the same question which has just been raised within a society will arise on a worldwide scale, namely who will be left to create the surplus to render all this possible. It would be best if the choice of a technology suitable for economic development were to fall on a kind of intermediate position, on an adapted technology which will be an improvement on the traditional technology but not, by simple transfer from the highly industrialized sphere, run too far ahead of it and thereby miss the adaptation in the economic and socio-cultural sense of the term.

To return to Schuman, Inkeles's bewildered fieldworker: those who will be involved in a production process must be able to see the point of the work demanded of them, in order to master corresponding behaviour patterns. The resistance and dislocation of which some are apprehensive will then not occur; instead, the new security and the greater wealth will have a positive effect. Inkeles's 'Psychosomatic Symptoms Test' did at least show that in the various countries in which it was applied, better results were achieved when a subject had had a longer experience of industrial situations: 'Men who had worked longer in industry did *not* thereby consistently acquire significantly more psychosomatic symptoms along with their seniority. Indeed, for the more successful men who had high skill and especially for those who had been able to buy more goods, there was a consistent and often significant tendency toward better adjustment' (Inkeles and Smith, 1974, 362). Most striking were the results of the study in India: '(Here) each step up the scale of increased exposure to modernizing influences brought with it a *decrease* in the number of psychosomatic symptoms' (263). This is confirmed by Naipaul, whose few hopeful experiences in India were with the new industries. Workers there 'Glory in their new skills. Men handling new machines, exercising technical skills that to them are new, can also discover themselves as men, as individuals. They are the lucky few' (1977, 74).

REMADE TECHNOLOGY

These are echoes of what in the recent past, in an earlier phase of development theory, was put on paper on the much discussed subject of entrepreneurship. In general economic theory the figure of the entrepreneur has always played a star role, and although recent reviews have been considerably less flattering, contemporary analyses still reveal traces of appreciation. In a study of labour-intensive production, Stewart, for instance, suggests that the approach exclusively from the factors labour and capital is insufficient: a third factor, 'managerial effort' needs also to be considered (1972, 102). It is after all management which decides how the production process will be organized and to what extent each factor of production will be employed.

Sen wonders, if one or other form of simple technology is so patently suitable, why then local entrepreneurs do not choose them of their own accord (1975, 12). In yet another publication Stewart complains that institutes specializing in adapted technology devise projects which often do not come to fruition because of the lack of entrepreneurs (1974, 41).

This is an old development-economical sore, which used to be called the 'capital illusion': the illusion namely that all would be well in the end if only sufficient funds were put at the disposal of the poor countries, a view which was finally discredited when it turned out that not all of the aid money was being spent, apparently because the receiving economy could not absorb it. Clark reports the tendency among entrepreneurs in developing countries to associate themselves with a foreign firm and leave the choice of technology to them, without further investigating the supply side to look for more suitable techniques (1975, 14). It is possible that here the thought figures that a firm becomes more important in development terms when its scale is increased, a view also defended by Schumpeter, the great theoretician of entrepreneurship. Industrial renewal, innovation, which lays the foundations for progress would, he thought, be better in the hands of a large firm which could supply the funds and manpower for research and bear the risks involved. But in the industrial sector of the rich countries small firms are still well represented: a recent study in West Germany, for instance, revealed that in this country there were still around 366,000 firms with less than ten employees. The journalist from 'The Times' reporting on the study attributes the greater wealth of Germany compared to Britain, where industry has concentrated in larger units, partly to this fact ('The Times', 21 October 1977). An American study showed that small businesses make an important contribution to the development of new techniques. On another occasion it was found that small firms applied certain technical innovations more readily than did the large corporations. The latter's research departments certainly knew about the new developments, but their application was delayed because the engineers who ran the show preferred to adopt a wait-and-see attitude (Bean, Schiffel and Mogee, 1975).

As discussed earlier, considerations of personnel policy also govern the choice for capital intensity. The decision for automation is occasionally taken on this basis in the industrial countries as well. Human relationships undeniably still exert a strong influence on productivity and controlling them remains fraught with problems; but if the work is done by a machine, the management can treat at least this factor as a constant. The personnel problems for a firm setting up a factory in a developing country are even greater because it now has to deal with people who have never before been in contact with a factory, let alone done factory labour, and will therefore have considerable difficulties in adjusting. A manager told Schumacher: 'People are difficult to control and make mistakes. Machines are easily controlled and do not make mistakes' (1975, 11).

In the rich countries there exists an established industrial climate, while in addition the methods of personnel management have been practised and refined ever since 1880, when Taylor made his first attempts at 'scientific management'. Many development economists have called for the transfer of this knowledge by means of management courses for potential entrepreneurs in the poor countries. But, as with the factor labour, more is involved than simply learning the specific skills. The re-socialization which Inkeles aims for - and the industrial sphere ideally lends itself to it - tries to strengthen the motivation on which action relies. When Tax speaks of Penny Capitalists, or Lloyd notes the tendency towards thrift, work and deferred gratification in the cities, both are in fact depicting the figure of the petty bourgeois familiar from the eulogies of the Protestant ethic (Lloyd, 1974, 348).

There are more resemblances. In the above-mentioned study the informal sector, pre-eminently the place of the small business, is praised as a kind of incubator in which budding entrepreneurs are nurtured. Persons may be found in that sector who stand out in that they endeavour to maintain their independence even when respected and protected jobs are available. An American survey of owners of small businesses showed that for most of them having a self-employed father had been decisive in their choice of occupation (Roberts, 1969, 229). 'To build up the self-respect and self-confidence of potential entrepreneurs and innovators in the developing countries is', in Jéquier's opinion, 'the prerequisite for a successful application of intermediate technology' (1976, 42).

But, as already stated, the stimulation of economic activity by favouring entrepreneurs is, at the moment, a vexed question. This is certainly due to the dislike which this group (and its practices) arouses in a growing number of left-wing economists. But in addition there is the suspicion that development through intervention of private entrepreneurs may steer expanding production in a direction which is considered undesirable in principle. In the absence of some board which supervises or directs on the basis of certain socially acceptable norms, the private investment decision may all too readily revert to a reaction to market prices, with personal gain as the primary goal. Admittedly, one cannot say that this system - capitalism - has operated wholly detrimentally in the rich countries, quite the contrary, but a number of side effects and an occasional main effect are by now deprecated by a wider circle, among development experts in any case. Moreover, the system leads to a selective preference for factors of production with a capital-intensive bias, and for reasons explained earlier this is to be avoided.

Where simple expansion of production is no longer the primary policy goal, the norms evidently need to be refined and supplemented, and it seems reasonable to consult the social sciences at this point, although of course the politicians will as always have the final say in the matter. The first question that arises is whether the professionals are able, on the basis of their presumed knowledge, to indicate the right direction. As far as the theory of entrepreneurship is concerned, this was expressly denied by one of its major exponents, Schumpeter; to think that development practice could be derived from theory he dismissed as a misapprehension. Contemporary theoreticians feel less constrained by such scientific relativism. Economists have been persuaded that the historically unprecedented acceleration of the economy in a number of countries in recent times is attributable to their particular know-how: 'We now have these things pretty much under control'. But now that the bubble for the time being seems to have burst, this confidence has been seriously shaken, and a whole range of opinions is being aired on the causes of stagnation. If, for instance, Stewart remarks that for a particular economy a precise set of goals must be formulated, which subsequently need to be balanced by adjudging certain weight coefficients to each and every one of them, then despite the meticulous care with which the exercise is carried out on paper, one wonders whether the ensuing prescriptions will be followed step by step and that thus the socio-economic problems will be gradually eliminated (1974, 33).

A balancing of policy goals can, furthermore, be seriously frustrated if they are by their very nature incompatible. Thus, getting as many people as possible some sort of income by creating employment will slow down the growth of income - another goal of development policy. It is not clear which target figures should be weighted and in what way. A dilemma of this kind becomes all the more pressing against the background of planning which is of necessity bound to a time dimension. The degree to which future generations will suffer as a result of (investment) decisions made today is a point often mooted in discussions on the environment. The idea of conservation is of course by its very nature oriented to the future. Now it is clear that any production requires the extraction of (in part non-renewable) natural resources, while at the same time it is to some extent attended by pollution. For the sake of the welfare of future generations, prudent use of natural resources and care for the environment are called for. In this case the present generation is expected to make a certain sacrifice, which consists of foregoing potential consumption, by being content with less production at higher - because environment-protective - costs. It doesn't seem reasonable to stop the present production processes altogether, for then there would not be any future generations. Although the conservationists do not say as much, there must be an optimum which balances the welfare of the present against that of the future. Had zero-growth been put into practice by the last generation, it might be said in hindsight that the optimum had obviously not as yet been reached, because the present generation is materially even better off. Yet from the point of view of finiteness it would have been more preferable to call a halt to the expansion of production at an earlier stage. But at what stage?

A satisfactory answer is possible only when we know how many generations there are still to appear on earth and which techniques they will choose to tap which resources. This knowledge we do not have; and for it to be rational the present act of choosing must set its horizons only as far as the present and at most the next generation. But the decision will be a difficult one even if it is restricted to this surveyable time span, because the issue is not whether a part of wealth is to be sacrificed, but rather whether poverty is alleviated or aggravated.

Whenever a development worker has the floor, the word Gandhi is bound to crop up sooner or later. An age-old undercurrent of thought - including Western thought - has resurfaced: the question 'What is the point of it all?' is put by economists and engineers, who in their professional capacity deal with means and on the whole have not regarded policy-making as within their competence. That there might be another, and, measured by different norms, a better form of society they remembered from their reading of utopian anthologies in their student days - names like Fourier or St Simon had stuck. But this was not considered applicable science. Knowledge was applied to the world of daily experience. Accumulation of knowledge was intended to help this world along the road that it had at one time turned down. It was not within the competence of the experts to decide whether this was the right direction or whether it was inevitable and had to be followed by everyone. But trained to solve any problem they encountered, they nevertheless set about the unfamiliar task. The peculiar formulae with which Schumacher supplied his latest publication are the outcome of this untrained thought which - however innocent - could lead to a new form of technocracy, in which the disconnected ideas of engineers and technicians would determine the life style of a society.

15 Development propensity

> 'When officials at an Asian University were asked who was concerned with the institution's pattern of output in relation to the country's projected needs, the reaction revealed astonishment that such a question should be raised at an institution of higher learning.'
> (Barnett)

Decisions on matters of technology need to be based on a prior policy choice. While formerly development economics displayed a marked tendency to put expansion of production above all else, in recent years the creation of employment has been given pre-eminence. The shift may be related to the rise in unemployment in the industrial countries, where during the great pre-war crisis the Keynesian school was taken by a similar mood. Keynes's recommendation to pay people to dig holes randomly and then fill them in again is not very pertinent to the poor countries, because they cannot call upon idle productive capacity to combat underconsumption. The strategy now concentrates more on the distribution of income, which occurs of course through the labour market. The greater the amount of labour drawn into production, the wider the spread of income over the population and the narrower the range of incomes. This conceivably is another policy goal, which in fact is in step with the strategy that gives primacy to employment creation. It also suits a policy aimed at modernization and served by the exposure of a large part of the population to the (temperate) industrial climate which labour-intensive techniques entail. It is in this way that Inkeles's demand for transparency and lucidity is best accommodated.

The principle of distribution discussed earlier whereby consumption is directly subsidized by capital-intensive production, is opposed by Sen on the grounds that it facilitates corruption (1975, 84). A more serious drawback seems to stem from the fact that this system - the practicability of which has in any case been seriously questioned - reduces a population to passivity and dependence, which is a far cry from being prepared for the new life patterns which development presupposes and from being spurred on to activity in this direction. Just as ergonomics in the industrial countries aims to adapt machines to the demands posed by the human body so that the operations physically suit the operators, it is equally desirable that new adapted techniques are likewise geared to the requirement that the workers be intellectually carried along in the direction facilitating further economic development. Inkeles's term 'modern' has perhaps too many advanced - or even post-industrial connotations to indicate what is expected of technology at this stage. It is preferable to speak of 'development-minded' to indicate which attitudes and conceptions can be promoted by means of technology and organization.

ADAPTED STRATEGY

The striving for economic independence as a pendant to political independence is, with deference to the Chinese model, often avowed as a principle of action. It was argued earlier that, quite apart from the question whether this particular policy is still pursued in China, this is a goal which runs counter to the development of a world economy in which national entities have become increasingly interwoven and in which, in extensive world trade, complementary specialization is increasing rather than decreasing. Nevertheless, it goes without saying that an advantage to be gained from a unique position must be exploited. This means firstly that the resources of a given country must be taken into account as possible starting points for industrial development. The focus on the European-American industrial sphere has rather prevented this, so that raw materials were imported to be processed in an industry which had also been imported. So plastic is used instead of wood, or in the building trade, the familiar corrugated iron sheets instead of bamboo. The trouble with raw materials is that presumed or even proven reserves in themselves do not present an economically relevant given. Some poor countries are called rich because they are known to have huge mineral reserves. But this potentiality only becomes economic actuality when the quality and quantity of the reserves have been ascertained with some accuracy and when the costs of extraction can be justified in terms of the expected returns. To solve such economic-technical problems, the poor country will again have to consult the feared multinationals, for they possess the required expertise.

In the first place the multinationals could be asked (as they have been repeatedly) to ensure that not only extraction but also processing take place in the poor country if at all practicable; and that in addition they do not apply a technique which is the most advanced and developed for an industrial country but rather that they follow an intermediate technique which will offer the largest possible employment. In certain cases this may not be technically feasible; the so-called process industries cannot but be capital-intensive. But at least the creation of indirect employment could, provided the project is adjusted to this policy consideration, be such that the investment will still have a marked effect on incomes. The 1975 UNCTAD study mentioned earlier showed that of the 159 foreign firms under scrutiny, 97 had a positive effect on the income of the local economy, in the sense that the social-economic value of output outweighed the sacrifices. Van Herel is right to point out, however, that in the calculations these sacrifices were costed at their market value, although over-invoicing is known to be common. But he still accepts that three out of every four factories contribute positively to income (1976, 34).

The effect of foreign investments could be broadened if the enclave character with which these industries are tainted is countered by a policy of establishing and encouraging complementary, labour-intensive factories. It has been found in the developing countries that an expanding industry tends to pass the results of rising labour productivity on to the workforce; over the years, wage an and salary costs have increased relatively to other costs. The same phenomenon appears in the countries of incipient industrialization: the foreign firms pay higher wages. This is partly due to pressure brought to bear by governments and trade unions. The foreign negotiators will have their domestic wage rates in the back of their minds, and against these the local wage demands will seem very modest indeed. Yet it is remarkable that these differences are reported from many poor countries, even though the negotiating positions are surely not the same everywhere. Stewart thinks that the higher wages are necessary to retain a stable workforce, that is, avoid high labour turnover and absenteeism. Furthermore: 'Required standards of health and hygiene, nutrition, punctuality, literacy and transport can only be achieved if wages are considerably higher than subsistence incomes' (1977, 73). The dual structure is thus in-built, and the striving for equality of income is frustrated.

Perhaps it should be borne in mind that the obverse of this is that the purchasing power of at least part of the population will increase; and this is essential for the emergence of an internal market in which the new goods can be sold and in which there is a demand for existing goods, agricultural produce for instance. It seems in any case unavoidable that the incomes of some sections of the population will rise faster than those of others, for the simple reason that investments, no matter how much they are directed to employment creation, are always restricted to certain groups. A modal rise in wages can only be expected when these groups start to overlap. The dual character of the economy will then resolve itself.

The question is whether, in the light of the rich countries' interest in the growing internationalization of commerce, the developing countries will in future only have the multinationals to turn to for their technology, adapted or otherwise. The well-known studies by Schmookler have shown that the big corporations raise the lion's share of the total research budget, but in recent years it has also been observed that less powerful firms have begun to tender for industrial projects in the Third World. The payments of royalties on semiconductors and automobile spare parts especially seem to indicate that the influence of the smaller firms is waxing (Helleiner, 1975, 180). The advent of small- or smaller-scale partners in development will in all probability play into the hands of the desired more limited framework of local industry. Yet it still seems unrealistic to think that foreign expertise will be able to develop an optimal intermediate technology for every infant industry.

UNADAPTED EXPERTISE

On the whole there has been little sign of a trend in this direction. Western technical-economic problems are different in kind, and research is after all carried out mostly by the big corporations, which thus try to gain an advantage over other equally capital-intensive corporations and supply a technically sophisticated market. According to Gustafson, 90 per cent of industrial research in the United States is directed to the development of new products or the refinement of existing ones (1962). This is more likely to harm rather than help the poor countries, because new consumer goods sometimes replace their own products: the synthetic fibre is but one example of a whole range of synthetic products which have had a ruinous effect on the markets for their natural equivalents.

From this viewpoint it is clear that Western industrial research, accounting as it does for 98 per cent of all research carried out in the world, only causes the poor countries to fall further behind. The Sussex group, which calculated the above figure, also found that less than 1 per cent of research in industrial countries is directed to the production problems of developing countries.

In 1969 the famous Pearson report proposed to raise this share to 5 per cent of state expenditure on research; a similar proposal of the United Nations went even further in that it suggested 5 per cent of overall research expenditure. An example of such research is Borlaug's into new seed strains, which has enlarged the agricultural production capacity of a number of tropical countries. As a matter of fact the resultant green revolution has thrown up so many new problems that the technician working on a (natural) scientific solution to problems of scarcity must be warned against undue optimism.

From the literature on adapted technology one gains the impression that a better adaptation is expected from solutions which have been devised in the poor countries themselves. But since in that part of the world only 0.2 per cent of gross national income is spent on research, it is for one thing quantitatively utterly inadequate, while doubts about its quality are also justified. Lewis is forthright: 'It cannot be denied that much if not most of the research going on in LDC's is irrelevant to the development needs of the countries and much too much of it is second-rate' (1972, 181).

Sagasti goes even further: 'The capacity for creating technology, or even for absorbing imported technology, is not present in most underdeveloped countries' (1973, 53). These authors explain this by the small number of local scientifically trained people and the enclave character of the knowledge which has been imparted to these few in Western countries or in any case in the Western tradition. Sagasti even warns against making funds available for scientific institutions in poor countries lest they feel encouraged to continue down the wrong path.

ADAPTED RESEARCH

It was pointed out earlier that the special technical capacities which have been developed in the industrial countries have become a cultural trait which now largely determines the character of these societies.

This peculiarly Faustian character of Western society had already come to the attention of Smith, who praised 'philosophers ... capable of combining the powers of the most distant and dissimilar objects'. He attributed the technological advances of the eighteenth century to this attitude of mind (Forbes, 1968, 22). Playfair, a Scot who helped to organize the Great Exhibition of 1851, intimated that the time had past when his country could fall back on its own resources: 'Industry must in future be supported, not by competition of local advantages, but by competition of intellects' (1852, 29). And indeed: imagine what would have happened to the European economy if technology had not developed any further after, say, the year 1900. More of the then existing tools and machines would have been built, but the returns on this investment would have diminished very quickly. Increasing the wealth of a growing population relies for a large part on the mutations in production technology which are the outcome of purposive research. The poor countries would be ill-advised to heed the Luddite echoes heard of late, calling for a stop to technology. Galtung et al.'s recommendation illustrates the fallacy: 'The other approach (is) that of finding more labour-intensive forms of production, winding down capital and research intensity' (1975, 535). The finding of the labour-intensive form, however, is not the chance hit of German *finden* but of *erfinden* (invention), if not, to remain with Mannheim, of *planen*.

As with other development-political decisions, this one must be taken in relation to other choices and the (objective) conditions under which development proceeds: rubber plantations are not laid out where there are no rubber trees; a labour-intensive tyre factory is not built where latex has to be imported. Because it is just impossible to control all variables, even the most elaborate plan is liable to what Hirschman calls the 'Principle of the Hiding Hand': the concealed, unexpected and unpredictable economic and social mechanisms which may thwart a particular economic impulse. But when the creation of wealth is guided by a well thought-out system of measures, less will be left to chance. Planning involves the search for adapted techniques that, given exogenous conditions and the goal envisaged, will maximize the stimulating effect of a production process by creating jobs and broadening industrial experience.

Galtung's simplistic 'winding down capital' does not contribute to this - the establishment of a local capital-goods industry would be more likely to do so! The engineers in the poor countries with no capital-goods sector are at the mercy of laboratories and university centres which are screened off from the routine of day-to-day production. It is obvious that the design of a new machine or the adaptation of an existing one is best served by close co-operation with the technicians who work in a factory where these machines are put together. In the rich countries, too, the most fruitful research is carried out in the capital-goods sector (Williams, 1973, 10). Stewart rightly refers to the 'learning and training dimension' involved here, and she considers the capital-goods sector essential to innovating activity (1977, 153). In a way this is a repetition of an earlier prescription of economic theory, which has been put into practice in the Soviet Union, namely that the build-up of the so-called heavy industry lays the foundation for future expansion of consumption. Except that now learning and motivation are given pride of place; this aspect was absent in the earlier model, which on the whole ignored the social dimension.

In the countries where technical capacity has expanded, a source of wealth has been tapped which unlike other factors of production is inexhaustible. Knowledge yields more knowledge, the source flows more abundantly the more it is exploited.

Internationalization of technical knowledge has produced in the poor countries an alien expertise suited only to the solution of inapposite problems. This technical capacity must be restored to its indigenous context.

The refinement of technical genius under inculcation of a national-economic goal occurs by means of a confrontation with local industrial problems: the scale of research is thus adapted to the scale of the need for research.

16 Development expertise

> 'It is not possible to dig a hole in a different place by digging the same hole deeper.' (de Bono)

That research should be made subservient to application is an idea which is anathema not only to the scientific elite of the poor countries. In Europe pure scientific research is also seen as a higher form of activity transcending worldly cares. Occasionally it is alleged that the culture of the Third World is 'literary': the educated there are verbally gifted and tend to consider a problem solved once its solution, or even just the problem itself, is put into words. Against this it is supposedly the maxim of 'action, not words' which guides the Western attitude. It is worth remembering in this context that until around 1800 the natural sciences, however pure, were not regarded very highly in European academic circles; that the discipline was first included in a university curriculum only in 1845 (namely at the Royal College of Chemistry in London) and that it was not offered at Oxford and Cambridge until much later. The histories of technology attribute the inventions which made the industrial revolution possible to clever handymen or 'hobby inventors', and they added the rider that these were illiterate barbers and grocers by profession. Jewkes explains this condescension by the lack of understanding of the professional academic for the self-taught man, but the former's awareness that the inventors did not uphold the intellectual values but, rather vulgarly, were trying to earn a living may also have played a role. Unqualified praise is only heaped on the scientist who is averse to all practicalities and is concerned solely with truth. Because even then some pragmatism cannot be dispensed with, it is pointed out that fundamental science in the pursuit of Knowledge yields as a secondary benefit knowledge which can be successfully applied elsewhere - 'spin-offs', as the contemporary jargon has it.

PRAXIS

Nevertheless, Atwood, a fellow of Trinity College, who taught philosophy at Cambridge around 1780, doubted whether it was fruitful for engineers to study mechanics: 'Machines of this sort owe their origin and improvement to other sources: it is from long experience of repeated trials, errors, deliberations (and) corrections, continued through the lives of individuals and by successive generations of them, that sciences, strictly called practical, derive their advancement' (Musson, 1972, 113). Engels voiced a similar opinion in a letter written towards the end of the nineteenth century: 'If a society has a need for a certain technology, then this does more to advance science than ten universities' (Rürup, 1974, 186). The contrary views are reconciled by Bernal, who qualifies them in his history of natural science as diachronic. During the early phase of industrialization, he maintains, the focus was on applied technology and scientists could learn something from the handymen; subsequently they were detached from it; in a more mature stage, when firms had expanded, research departments were set up where scientists, sometimes in freedom, sometimes with a detailed brief, carried out their work in the service of production. 'Many people', he remarks, 'still think of science as it appeared to be in the nineteenth century, as the product of individual men of genius, instead of, as it now is, a highly organized new profession closely linked with industry and government' (1969, 4).

At a congress in 1976 on intermediate technology Schumacher expressed his apprehension that the academics would only deal with problems at a theoretical level: 'They take it up. They solve it. And then they file it away' (TOOL, 1976, 21). He draws the conclusion that research on adapted technology should be carried out where it is to be applied, in the immediate vicinity of the project.

This is also urged by Streeten: 'What matters is the development of "indigenous scientific capability". R & D abroad is no substitute for R & D at home' (1972, 228).

But European and American science has plunged into the study of the problem of development. Almost half a century ago, when the world was not yet divided into three according to levels of economic development, Schumpeter wrote in his classic 'Capitalism, Socialism and Democracy' that, with all due respect to left-wing intellectuals, he could not help thinking that their enthusiasm for the revolution would fast dissipate if it turned out that they would have no role to play in it. Keynes's hope that economists would become active as lowly craftsmen, unnoticed and useful like a dentist, has not come true; Pickett et al.'s image of the 'jet-set advocates of labour-intensive processes' seems accurate (1974, 54). 'The Economist' is taken aback by the army of observers, ideologues, professional revolutionaries, fashionable economists and other 'third-world bores' swarming out all over the tropical world or devoting themselves to 'consciousness-raising' at home (11 March 1978, Survey 3). Streeten, often on the road himself, takes offence at the beautiful villas in Bellagio, Ditchley Park, Bürgenstock and Königswinter, where well-fed discussion groups spawn new ideas on the struggle against poverty (1974, 8).

DENOMINATION

The churches have also jumped at the chance to bear witness to their feelings for their fellow men. In the Netherlands, where progressiveness often appears in the guise of the effusive young clergyman, a conference paper on intermediate technology concluded that 'We have to continue to sell the gospel' (Korthals Altes, 1975, 15). The pride in all the good being done in the colonies, still inculcated into the previous generation during their schooldays, has made way for a feeling of guilt, which is absolved by the transfer of aid money. In addition, scapegoats have to be found: it is the local self-aggrandizing elite and the intransigent powers-that-be here at home who have obliged. Allahwerdi quite seriously declares a holy war on Western industry (1974, 267). Total revolution is called for, preferably on the Chinese model. Because immediate results can hardly be expected at home, there is a notable tendency to plead for revolution elsewhere. The staffs of Western universities and of the 279 institutes for intermediate technology which have meanwhile sprung out of the ground, together are a broadly based vested interest in the war on poverty.

Yet despite all the scientific work, there remains a tendency towards oversimplification and abstraction. The former is underpinned ideologically by the assumption that all problems are caused by imperialist exploitation; the latter by the amalgamation of the more than 100 developing countries which form the Third World into a single category. If the ideal of self-sufficiency, also prescribed for these countries, is to be meaningful, it will surely have to have a different content in Korea than in Kenya, in Haiti than in Thailand, in Colombia than in India. And it is difficult to see why the views of the Western consciousness-raisers should be incorporated into this content, for they derive their priorities from their own changing culture, where ten years ago economic growth was still the ideal. The norms of Western society change so quickly that long-term projects such as the supersonic passenger plane - an enormously expensive but advisedly chosen investment - are assigned to the dustbin even before the aircraft are ready to fly. The poor countries cannot be expected to realize their independence in conformity to a norm which has been devised as the latest thing by one or other European aid-giving institution. At a conference in Singapore, Wertheim was rebutted in this vein when he reminded the academics present of their duty to help the masses in their struggle to put the landlords and capitalists to the sword: 'Fine for you, professor', someone interjected, 'but I'm the sausage that's going to be fried in the fire - though I am neither landlord nor capitalist.' Streeten, who recounts the incident, adds that agitating for changes in a faraway land is a relatively innocent radical pastime.

But any other, even a more conservative, form of international aid will also contain a normative factor - for it is inherent in the concept of transfer that the receiving country is provided with a cultural element which it lacks. Economists all too easily talk about technology as if it were a neutral phenomenon; but if one recognizes the profound social effects which technology has wrought in the culture that gave birth to it, it will become clear that the transfer of even a modified technical attainment from one culture to another will only aggravate already existing problems. When President Truman proclaimed the aid programme known as 'Point Four', the great lever that was to lift the stagnating economies off the ground, no one doubted its beneficial effectiveness. Kindleberger summarized the message as follows: 'The underdeveloped countries could be made to catch up with the rest of the world through the simple communication to them of the secrets of advanced technology' (1965, 76).

A breakthrough in the technology of the industrial world is often found to have unexpected applications and stimulate another sector of the economy. Defenders of the value of space travel adduce such spin-offs to justify the enormous investments. Yet the transfer of technology is not always easy even within the industrial world. The spin-offs are a form of horizontal imitation, whereby a technique that was originally developed for a particular production process is made serviceable to another process, by adaptation if necessary. More problematic is the vertical transfer, whereby a technique initiated in pure-scientific research is followed up in applied research and finally in production itself. The line does not always run from the general to the specific either: some techniques are system-specific, some even specific to the system adopted in one particular firm. Seeing that the literature on the subject considers the phases of transfer within the industrial sphere to be a problem which merits serious analysis, it would be very odd indeed if the transfer outside would not encounter additional adversity.

COMMUNICATION

Streeten consequently talks of the 'communications gap' which he has observed in addition to the 'suitability gap': even if a particular technique is in a technical sense judged to be perfectly suited to application in a particular situation in a country, there still remains the problem of closing the gap which, to put it in psychological terms, separates apperception from perception (1972, 45). Knowing how it could be done is not the same as actually doing it that way. Because technology is so much embodied in tangible equipment, in what are pre-eminently elements of material culture, the analyses of the transfer process will deal with the human factor, that is people's ability to use the equipment properly, only in the second instance. But even if only the actual operations have to be learned, the success or failure of the transfer still seem largely dependent on communication. *It is really only possible to speak of a successful transfer when the receiving country has acquired the capability to develop under its own steam the techniques most suitable for the production processes under its own control.*

Stewart and Morawetz note that (small-scale) Chinese industry only got off the ground after the Soviet Union had withdrawn its technical aid. The example of Rhodesia has already been referred to. Its economy, Hoogvelt observed, benefited rather than suffered from the economic sanctions imposed after UDI (1973). In recent years international aid has been decried because it perpetuates the state of dependence; it should be added perhaps that it may also hinder technical self-activity. The Sussex Manifesto attaches great significance to this factor: 'Indigenous scientific capability is essential for creating the capacity to produce in the developing countries' (1974, 10).

A transplant, with adaptation if necessary, seems easier; and as was shown earlier, the kind of international aid which would enable the poor countries to carry out their own research has accounted for a very small part of the total aid. And since the countries themselves are in no position to allocate the required funds, it can be said that an indigenous capability to design appropriate techniques or even adapt inappropriate ones for local use is almost wholly absent. True, in a number of developing countries there are science councils and similar institutions, but studies have shown that their impact has been extremely limited (Cooper, 1974, 53).

The academics' aforementioned aversion to getting involved in pedestrian activities which research into small-scale industry entails has tended to sour such relations as do exist with universities. Student research in turn tends to be fruitless owing to the bias in the curriculum towards the modern sector - where the successful graduates eventually hope to find a job. When they have to compete with graduates from foreign universities, their knowledge and experience should not be inferior, the more so because the coveted positions will be abroad. It was found in Turkey that most research was performed for the purpose of inclusion in doctoral theses. Its subject will be determined by the level of knowledge which at the time is considered the norm in foreign universities. In Kenya engineers from the University of Nairobi did concern themselves with local problems, though only those in the capital-intensive sector. Even in Ireland, where scientific staff is more plentiful and the National Science Council promotes research on problems of the home market, the smaller businesses are largely denied any technical information, while the foreign establishments, enticed with subsidies and tax concessions, prefer to let their parent companies carry out the research. In the Netherlands the Central Organization for Applied-Scientific Research (TNO) also has little to do with small businesses.

Much has been written in development literature about the need for expanding educational facilities and thus raising local expertise to the desired level. Where the number of graduates from home universities did indeed expand, as in India for instance, a surplus was soon created and higher degrees far from ensured employment in local industry. Since at that time demand exceeded supply in Europe, the phenomenon of the 'brain drain' manifested itself. Complaints about this loss were silenced when the migration came to an end as soon as job opportunities dried up. In the meantime international research institutes have scored important successes: the Rice Institute in the Philippines, the Institute for Tropical Agriculture in Nigeria and the Potato Research

Centre in Peru - all financed out of development funds - spring to mind.

This has prompted the suggestion, included in the World Action Plan of the United Nations for instance, that similar institutions be set up in the industrial field. Research could be initiated resulting in special techniques suited to particular production processes in various countries. The adaptation of existing, but in their present form less suitable, techniques was to be carried out. Graduates of the applied technical sciences from developed and developing countries would be brought together and each institution might concentrate on the specific problems of its own region. But as far as communication between people is concerned, it is wise not to rely altogether on what look like expertly and rationally conceived structures. 'It is hard enough to gain real communication within the homogeneous background of one's own family' (Peters, 1975, 75). Any transfer in a less intimate context will have to overcome much greater obstacles; in incidental international co-operation it is a wonder that any statement is ever understood more or less as it was meant. In the light of the above-mentioned approach of fostering the attitude required for industrial activity by a conscious adjustment of the industrial apparatus, another proposal seems to offer better chances, namely that of the pilot plant. A report from the Agency for International Development (AID), in which the activities of fifty research institutes in developing countries are discussed, calls the 'demonstration pilot plant ... the major potentially successful link that joins industrial research institutes to the industrial development process' (Lewis, 1972).

In cases where research yields encouraging results for the kind of industrial application advocated here, Schiavo-Campo and Singer urge the setting-up of a pilot plant in the prospective location of the factory proper. There the teething troubles which affect every production process in its initial phases could be combated. But equally importantly, 'Pilot factories should be designed to get the bugs out of people who are expected to run commercial production' (1970, 132). Philips, the Dutch electronics giant, has gained some experience with a project of this type. In Utrecht it has been running a kind of parent pilot plant which has set up subsidiaries in more than twenty countries. All these small factories make electronic consumer goods in small batches and for a limited market. Again Ramaer sees the reasons for the success of the project in the human factor: 'Philips happened to have a man with an idea and the initiative to create such a plant' (1976, 6). Problems that arose could be referred back to the firm's experts in practical industrial management. 'It could therefore continually check its ideas with existing reality'. The management of the pilot plant was nevertheless wholly autonomous and the location, at some distance from corporate headquarters in Eindhoven, was chosen to forestall excessive interference. Ramaer did not put any major difficulties arising in the Third World subsidiary down to technical hitches but to the 'communication gaps (which) had to be bridged by more extensive training and more intensive personal contact' (1976, 7).

When writers analyse the problems which can bedevil pilot plants, they name technical factors above all: inferior quality of the available raw materials, different geographic and climatic circumstances, smaller scale of production. It is remarkable that, drawing on a long experience with a technically relatively complicated product in a great number of countries, Ramaer concludes that it is communication, the human factor in other words, which decides success or failure.

Earlier, Streeten's illuminating distinction between the 'suitability' and the 'communications gap' was referred to. Techniques can be made suitable - perhaps there are even some in existence already which require little or no adaptation; but a simple registering, the compilation of a technical catalogue which has been advocated, does not bridge the gap between countries in which large groups have been prepared for and have grown up with technical achievements and other countries in which industrial technology is brought as an alien cultural element. Complaints about wrong operation, neglect of machines, neglect of even simple maintenance such as lubricating or changing oil, expressed in the phrase cited earlier on: 'Give us the jobs and we'll finish the tools', hint at adjustment problems in the human rather than in the technical sphere. In the long, slow development of technology in the industrial countries the attitudes of successive generations have evolved during the course of development and towards the demands of mechanized or automated production. Technical problems, teething troubles of a new means of production, are approached in a mood of 'problem-solving' behaviour; its opposite, 'problem-shelving behaviour', is rather less prevalent. It is interesting that the historiography of technology unintentionally records a secondary social phenomenon, namely the emergence of technical clubs in the early stages of technical development. Groups of 'projectors' and 'innovators' apparently felt the need for response, for discussion with like-minded experts.

Burns deals with the role of these clubs: '(Spreading) the new learning to ever-widening circles; technology became something of a fashion' (1956, 47). All these new things annoyed some people, which surfaced in Dr Johnson's remark that 'everyone is running wild after innovation'. If this was to go on, he predicted that the condemned would eventually have to be hanged according to a new procedure. (Indeed, the guillotine could be seen as the technical response to the productivity demand entailed by the French Revolution.) In a time when technology is in bad odour it is salutary to remember that the first signs of machine production were generally welcomed, so much that composers accepted commissions to write special hymns for the opening of new factories (Duller, 1973, 4). This enthusiasm has slowly dissipated, though it should be remembered that it also emerged slowly, that many generations in the industrial countries have undergone a habituation which Marx described as a modification of 'consciousness'; and that it is unlikely that such a social process in the countries where this transformation is a derivative will be effected simply by putting forward a technical catalogue. Technical knowledge is now so massive that computer storage is a logical step in order to improve classification and accessibility of information. But it is doubtful whether a data bank, even one geared to adapted techniques, will solve development problems.

Boon says rightly that the developing countries cannot choose the appropriate technology if the choices are not clearly outlined (1976, 731). The special centres for intermediate technology may help to bridge the 'suitability gap' and narrow the 'communications gap': *but if a transfer is to be successful it is imperative that proper attention is paid to the learning process which initial industrialization entails*. International information centres, as proposed by the Council of Europe and welcomed by UNCTAD and UNIDO, provide excellent opportunities for putting on show the technical options, but exposition cannot ensure that they will actually be used. As Stewart put it incisively: 'Even the idea what the needs are is a required innovation' (1974, 36). The idea of a pilot plant was suggested by UNIDO for information banks to be started for four different industrial sectors. Iron and steel, fertilizer, processing of agricultural products and agricultural equipment would each have their own centres which would gather information relevant to their own special technical problems and test it in a projected application. A next step would be to supervise the application and to ensure not only organizationally but also managerially that a production method which was adjudged suitable for technical reasons also had the best chance, once grafted, of being accommodated by the recipient structure and survive - a promising new industrial branch.

REPERCUSSIONS

The pilot plant is a logical continuation of the collection of technical data for experimental purposes. And, by carefully recording social repercussions, eventually a level of knowledge can be reached which Inkeles could not attain, but which is crucial to define a future development strategy.

The behaviour of investors will then no longer be dominated only by the transfer code drawn up by Pugwash, UNCTAD and United Nations, which tries to protect the interests of the poor country; it will also be guided by positive considerations as to the manner in which an investment can be made to reach the result which is desirable as well from the point of view of the investor. The stage of maturity which technical development and rise in income have brought about in a number of industrial countries has also thrown some of the sectors where previously the growth was most pronounced, into disarray. For the sake of preserving jobs, the life of the shipbuilding, steel and car industries, which make losses that even if expressed per worker are impressive enough to be front page news, is drawn out month by month by means of enormous subsidies. The production cycle from innovation to maturity was discussed earlier. Development runs gradually from the small-scale beginning to mass production of a standardized product. The setting-up of subsidiaries in economically less developed areas becomes attractive for the original manufacturers. As the prices had to be lowered to maintain sales in a saturated home market, and as labour costs were rising, the low wage level of the poor country becomes attractive, while the product sold locally will probably suit the lower phase of development of the receiving economy.

In the meantime the rapid development of industry in countries like Taiwan and South Korea has upset the traditional centre-periphery relationship of the radical scheme. Textiles, shipbuilding and even electronics industries in the centre are getting into trouble as a result of the activities unleashed in countries which were presumed to be hopelessly dependent. This in fact means that economic development is taking place, which is after all what the underdeveloped countries were initially aiming for. Perhaps this goal can be reached in a labour-intensive way - particularly where (parts of) production processes are transferred from industrial countries for wage-cost reasons. As explained earlier, this is the aim, but the goal of expansion of production so that consumption per head will increase must remain primary (in the long term if nothing else). A recent study on productivity in agriculture has shown that it will not be possible to feed the world population with labour-intensive methods, which moreover were also found to do greater damage to the environment (Oort, 1978, 32).

In the usage of yesterday's progressive theology it may be said that this touches upon a marginal situation, but one in which the dialogue of the ideologues must be silenced. No ideology argues that hunger is desirable. Here we have indeed a 'basic need', followed by clothing and housing, whose satisfaction transcends all ulterior considerations. At this level there is no scope for the experiment with 'creativity', the small scale for its own sake. If more electrical energy is needed for a project than can be generated by a windmill in the back garden, then a power station will have to be built. The sophisticated worry that smoking chimneys, once a symbol of wealth, also mean pollution need not for the time being bother those who are pursuing a policy of expansion of consumption. The poor countries can at this stage not be troubled with Western traumas, which, incidentally, have not prevented Western development. 'What kind of society and human beings are we planning for?', asks Agosin (1976, 18). The objection which Mannheim raised when he put the same question to the European countries in the 1930s is 'Who plans the planner?'. Or to put it more strongly: who will here, on the silk cushion of prosperity, decide what should happen there?

The authors of a recently published development-economic textbook warn that 'Governments may not be willing to pursue the "national interest" as we define it' (Lall and Streeten, 1977, 219).

Indeed, they claim the right of definition for themselves. The same book reiterates 'the profound disillusionment of development economics'. Here the scientists' overestimation of their own ability avenges itself. It was they who put themselves forward as 'social engineers' while their discipline was not yet in a position to explain and clarify the development process. That people in government offices in the poor countries occasionally listen has less to do with a reverence for expertise than with an appreciation for the development funds, which tend to be allocated only after expert advice has been sought. In this stage of knowledge, little more than informed personal opinion can be offered. A number of development workers have come to espouse the personal opinion that industrialization (on Western lines) is an evil and that increase of consumption should not be recommended as a matter of course. This may go down very well in a 'personal growth' encounter group, it does not in an Indian planning office. 'Not many can be rescued from the nullity of pre-industrial India', Naipaul says sadly, because industrialization cannot proceed rapidly enough to provide the unemployed and poor masses with work and income (1977, 74). Industrialization is also thought to disrupt traditional social patterns, causing social order to break down, disorientation, degeneration and insecurity. For these very reasons the expansion of the industrial sector is sometimes rejected. Yet it was precisely the industrial workers in six developing countries who were found to have a better state of (mental) health than those who had remained outside the factories in correspondingly greater poverty and uncertainty about their future. In India in particular, 'each step up the scale of increased exposure to modernizing influences brought with it a decrease in the number of psychosomatic symptoms. The one clear-cut result, therefore, argued that if exposure to modernizing influences (i.e. industry) had had any effect, it was to improve personal adjustment' (Inkeles and Smith, 1974, 263). Naipaul provides the explanation: 'Indian poverty is more dehumanizing than any machine' (1977, 170).

When Lewis published one of the first textbooks on the Third World, he already encountered the problem of human happiness. Does the creation of material wealth contribute to it or detract from it? His solution is still often cited and is typically a product of economic thought: 'The advantage of economic growth is not that wealth increases happiness but that it increases the range of human choice' (1957, 420). But it is not that simple. Once it is decided to give priority to economic development, admittedly the number of economic means of gratification from which the consumer can choose will increase depending on the success of the policy, but the choice for a different organization of society is in fact restricted by the policy chosen. To put the case in extreme form (and in the economic terminology of alternative costs): perfect conviviality is the lost paradise, for whose loss we are compensated with material wealth. In deep poverty there is no alternative to the basic choice, but making the choice will cut off alternative paths up to the point where basic scarcity has been pushed back to such an extent that going any further becomes a less and less important consideration for the majority of the population. Here lies the crux: those who are 'surfeited with honey' and no longer taste the 'sweetness' are less appreciative of the busyness of the bees (Henry IV, part 1, act III, scene III). Or: social perception of the economic problematic shifts with the increase in material wealth.

Established economic theory tended to deny the possibility of individual comparisons of wealth. In terms of all kinds of observable criteria one economic subject could be better off than another, but because his soul was closed to scientific inquiry there was no way to determine whether he actually was wealthier. Because the need of the consumer apparently does not end when the saturation point seems near, it is possible to argue that dissatisfaction - and thus (subjective) absence of wealth - can be as strong at a higher level as at a lower. Even if this were a rule, it is unlikely that it will be equally valid along the whole continuum from poor to rich. Below an objectively more or less ascertainable (hunger) line at a point where non-satisfaction of needs endangers subsistence, it is clear that any expansion of means of gratification will increase both wealth and welfare. It is the aim of intermediate technology to achieve this with means of production which, despite the poverty, are supplied by the poor countries themselves and which fit in both the economic and the social environment. Wage and machine costs, productivity and income effects are measurable; the adaptation to social institutions, to the norms and behaviour of the people who are affected by the strategy, is a challenge to which a response must now be found.

17 Development possibility

> 'Technology is sometimes man's chief hope and at other times his main fear.' (Johnson)

'We are now in a period of transition.' This oft-heard saying contains an element of threat, but also one of comfort: the first raises a worrying question 'Where will it take us' the second assuages this apprehension, albeit with a sigh: 'There is an end to everything - to joy as well as misery.'

Even here some sort of intermediate position is conceivable, as is evident from one of the most recent 'alternative' books by De Hastings, who not only describes our planet as crisis-prone but also as crisis-proven, thereby revealing himself as the man of mature judgment (1980, 134). Meanwhile, no sane person would quibble with the description of our era as one of transition, for the excellent reason that each era is of necessity preceded by an earlier and followed by a later one; between these two periods there is another which separates the first from the last; this, then, is the period of transition.

In an unstable society successive periods differ markedly from each other; yet, in retrospect, it will be possible to identify one that unites elements of the preceding sequence with characteristics of the next. If the succession proceeds dialectically, so that the element of contrast predominates, then the nature of transition becomes that much more salient. Thus Mannheim in the 1930s could speak of a 'Zeitalter des Umbaus'. That the present era is full of contradictions is evident from the quotation by the economist Johnson, at the beginning of this chapter: technological society is dependent on, but also in awe of technology. Of the latter, E. (No-Growth) Mishan's phrase is most poignant: 'The thorny path of industrialization leads only to the wasteland of Subtopia' (1960, 194).

THE ROARING SIXTIES

The crisis years preceding the war were characterized to a large measure by nostalgia, especially in America, a harking back to the so-called roaring twenties, a wistfulness that never really disappeared and that has recently been revived in dress and furniture styles. 'Those were the days.'

But what, in a previous chapter, was called the deuxième belle époque, was, all things considered, a better time. Not only because, unhindered by prohibition, one could freely indulge in liquor and generally in the sort of pleasures which were previously considered reprehensible, but now were sanctioned by the 'permissive society'; but above all because there was a far greater prosperity which was moreover enjoyed by a far greater number of consumers. It is not purely fanciful therefore to suggest that the 1960s will go down in history as even more 'roaring' than the 1920s. The abandon with which a generation succumbed to consumerism, welcomed by publicists such as Kahn, previously discussed, Zahn, already forgotten, and Van Zuthem, who questioned the credibility of our economic order (because the basis of that order - scarcity - had long been overcome!) may well be cause for a future generation to relapse once more into nostalgia. For our economic ideas are once more dominated by finiteness, and we are once again confronted with the problem of scarcity as much as we ever were (Van Zuthem, 1969, 13).

The victory of the democratic allies in the Second World War has been ascribed in part to the research efforts of the 'back room boys' whose discoveries furnished them with increasingly effective means of defence and attack. After the defeat of Germany, Italy and Japan, the United States became the undisputed world power - militarily and politically, but above all technologically. The American myth of limitless opportunity at last seemed a reality. While the other nations, the victors and the vanquished, had been impoverished, the American economy emerged intact from the conflict and indeed stronger than ever before. The rest of the world lay in ruins and naturally technology was called upon to expedite reconstruction and subsequently to take up arms against world poverty.

'Technology was regarded as the key to everything desirable in the way of human betterment ...' (Johnson, 1975, 116). The same applied to what was looked upon as economically desirable: 'The use of new technology is one of the main engines of economic growth' (Hill and Utterbeck, 1979, 1).

When against this prevailing thought the problem of the economic underdevelopment of the Third World manifested itself, the same remedy was recommended: here, too, modern technology would be the panacea. The enticements of large-scale operations described in an earlier chapter once more conjured up promises of prosperity.

Where, in the preceding discussion, so much attention was focused on comparative scientific climatology and the limited relevance of the diverse intermediate technologies proposed was shown, the time has come to pass judgment on this new direction in economic thinking, in a sanguine attempt to approach objectivity. This question is all the more pressing since the potentially disadvantageous effects of the strategy have been treated at length in these pages.

We have seen how, in poor countries, cheap products for mass consumption can by their very nature only be mass produced, while the production of goods destined for a consumer elite can be very labour intensive. Furthermore, the striving to save on capital costs was shown to have a negative effect on the ratio between investment and output as shown in the capital-coefficient. It was also established that the primary aim for several 'development decades', namely the raising of national income, is not necessarily served by the small-scale approach. Moreover, following such guide lines consistently would mean either having to do without a number of goods or having to import them. Some products which are vital for independent development, might not be manufactured locally at all, at least not of the requisite quality. Thus, that section of the market would be left to foreign enterprise. Small wonder that the 'Small is Beautiful' credo finds little favour in the Third World. What must they make of our admiration for the Chinese People's Republic, strangely oblivious of its feverish acquisition of modern machinery, which even before the recent policy change was surreptitiously being supplied by Hong Kong. Western admiration, however, is exclusively reserved for barefoot doctors, acupuncture, mini blast furnaces and biogas. Spokesmen for poor countries view this with suspicion. The Chinese achievements in the field of nuclear armaments and rockets remain unacknowledged, yet it is precisely those that most command the respect of technologically impotent nations. The sudden preference in the industrial West for the small, the delicate and the natural is looked upon elsewhere with astonishment. Are the developing nations being dissuaded from establishing their own petrochemical industries for ecological reasons or because the industrial powers would rather hold on to their monopoly of those products? Where the green revolution succeeded it was not, after all, because of small-scale bio-dynamic agriculture, but because use was made, on a massive scale, of agro-chemicals and diesel oil, 'improving the nutrition levels of many of India's poorest people. If the Third World is not going to be self-reliant in its food needs, it can forget about clothing, health care, housing and education, indeed about everything else' (Parthasarathi, 1979 , 36).

On the other hand, the undeniable advantages of small-scale operations also became apparent in the previous chapters: a limited investment may employ many more people, and if the industry is set up so that the workers can acquire something of the productive frame of mind, such a project may well be more conducive to development than could be deduced from the micro-economic effect alone. The sacrifice of a possibly higher product price would then be justifiable and that the consumer has to pay more, can be weighed against the advantage that existing traditional industries, producing related articles, are not immediately put out of business. Moreover, the alarming growth of Third World cities, due to a continuous influx of people from the rural areas, which can no longer support them, will be decelerated; employment opportunities spread throughout these areas could adjust to the agricultural work pattern to absorb a constant or fluctuating labour surplus. The learning process that accompanies all sustained development is best promoted by linking up the new skills with those traditionally at hand in the area, as was already advocated. In this context Johnson notes that European agriculture in the past has known long periods of steadily increasing productivity which he explains in terms of that selfsame learning process: 'individually microscopic improvements in traditional techniques and ... in primitive tools'. And this process was repeated during the development of the European steel industry (Johnson, 1975, 2). *Doing is the best way of learning*. 'If learning performance is to improve, the stimuli situations must themselves be evolving' (Kingston, 1977, 42).

Leibenstein opts for a similar approach in his latest book on X-efficiency (1978). He reverts to the economic behaviour ascribed to man by traditional theory: man's actions are assumed to be rational, which, in this context, implies that a technical innovation which increases productivity is recognized as such and is consequently taken up as soon as possible. But optimal efficiency in this mechanistic sense is found only in thermo-dynamics, as laid down in the famous Second Law. Economic decisions made by human actors fall short of such predictable constancy. The difference between the optimum and the actual relationship of input to output is expressed by the degree of 'X-efficiency', as Leibenstein calls it. A similar manufacturing process in diverse countries with identical inputs in identical allocations, may well produce different outputs. Theory does not recognize such discrepancies because it assumes that, under equivalent objective conditions, the same decision will invariably be taken. The expert, steeped in such theoretical assumptions, will have specific expectations concerning the output of a given investment; he is not prepared for any substantial negative deviation. Nor does he approach the chosen method of production from the point of view of a strategy which would eventually narrow the frustrating gap. Leibenstein aims to improve the X-efficiency by applying the 'learning by doing' principle (117). On-the-job learning effects, in his opinion, will eventually even favourably affect production processes elsewhere in the economy: 'Some firms may raise the quality-effort standard and make efficient labour available to other firms' (118).

In this technological strategy, adjustment to indigenous idiosyncrasy is made on location, in the developing country proper, as opposed to the laboratory in the remote atmosphere of the donor. There the expertise, the learning and the goodwill are readily available but, in the words of Sagasti, it is a matter of creating an 'endogenous science and technology base ... in order to escape from the conditions of underdevelopment' (1979, 20). It is all very well to reflect profoundly on the socio-cultural context: here we have a concrete situation which offers a starting point for active political and socio-economic change. Sagasti lays so much stress on the presence or absence of an indigenous ability to generate technology that he reduces the dichotomy developed-underdeveloped to the availability of an 'endogenous scientific and technological base' versus the reliance on an 'exogenous scientific and technological base'. In Europe, that endogenous base was established in the course of the seventeenth century, drawing on Hellenistic sources via the Roman empire, with Arabic additions. Sagasti does not suggest that such processes were disturbed in other cultures by colonialism; but he does ascribe to it the fact that science and industry in former colonies have developed separately. 'The pursuit of science did not grow roots ... it acquired a fragmentary and imitative character, divorced from the production sphere' (17). The conclusion is unavoidable: development efforts must aim at the self-reliance of the technological resources in the Third World. Such know-how will be brought to bear on the problems posed by the adapted technology of their own industries. *There is no other choice.* That is made particularly clear in Zimmerman's work on the subject.

Zimmerman too dismisses the views of that school of economic development, now already considered traditional, which, during the 1950s, advocated the elevation of poorer nations through rapid industrialization. As already discussed: the problem of poverty was considered to be soluble within 20 years, by applying Nurkse's 'wave of capital investments' to Hirschman's strategic points with optimal 'linkages' so that Rostow's 'self-sustained growth' could be heralded and 'the age of high mass consumption' announced to the world. If this potent medicine from the West were administered in ample quantities, the twentieth century's challenge would soon be met.

Zimmerman points out that, with this strategy, the ex-colonies are told in no uncertain terms that their future prosperity is totally dependent on the benevolence of the mother country: both the money and the know-how had to come from the West. It was soon realized that the poor nations did have at least one possible source of prosperity that could be tapped cheaply: namely the abundant, perhaps even superfluous, agricultural labour. Gauged by optimal forms of productivity the tropical agricultural labour force shows a surplus. This potential prosperity factor should not be wasted: particularly since labour, unlike capital, cannot be stored up for later use. 'Activating this idle labour should be top on the agenda of every development plan' (1975, 413).

But the optimism which accompanied that recommendation some twenty years ago has evaporated. The labour shortage in industrial nations, at one time compensated by the importation of migrant workers, has meanwhile turned into redundance. Several explanations have been given for this reversal: e.g. that industrial growth is crippled by an increase in government expenditure; that rising incomes favour the service industries so that the tertiary sector is growing at the expense of the secondary; but above all that the expansive investment in industry has caused a relatively diminishing demand for labour. England, historically the first industrial nation, was still experiencing a 16 per cent growth in the industrial sector between 1965 and 1977, while employment dropped by 15 per cent during the same period (Blackaby, 1969, 6). Industry's ability to absorb labour became less as technology advanced; no wonder, since every effort was made to save expensive labour during the design stages of new machinery.

That statement clearly demonstrates the inexpedience of the previously recommended strategies for industrial development for backward economies. However powerful Nurkse's 'wave of capital investment', with modern technology it is inconceivable that the enormous labour resources of the Third World will ever be adequately employed, let alone exhausted. By way of confirmation, Zimmerman introduces the concept of the RIEOR: the relative incremental employment output ratio. This is the quotient of the percentage increase in employment opportunities during a given period, and the percentage increase in the production index in the same period. Table 4 gives figures for twenty countries for the period 1963-72.

TABLE 4

Denmark	0.06	Finland	0.24
West Germany	0.08	El Salvador	0.24
Japan	0.11	Hungary	0.26
France	0.13	Canada	0.26
Italy	0.14	Zambia	0.27
Belgium	0.15	Yugoslavia	0.30
Spain	0.21	Poland	0.30
Norway	0.23	Israel	0.31
Philippines	0.23	Australia	0.36
United States	0.24	South Korea	0.40

From these figures it is evident that twelve of the twenty countries have a RIEOR of between 0.20 and 0.30, averaging approximately 0.25. In the underdeveloped nations, no more than 20 per cent of the labour force is employed in the industrial sector, so that an industrial expansion of 1 per cent would at the most have a 0.05 per cent effect on the employment market. It is, however, assumed that if industrial expansion provides one extra job, the service sector will also expand to provide one more job. The total effect, therefore, of a 1 per cent industrial expansion would then mean an increase in employment opportunities of 0.10 per cent. But even that still means that to increase employment by 1 per cent, the industrial sector must expand by 10 per cent.

The annual population increase in the Third World is between 2.5 and 3 per cent. *It is clear that such an increase in the potential labour force cannot possibly be absorbed by modern, large-scale industrialization. The strategy of the 1950s is unworkable.*

One may well ask whether the strategy today suits the wealthy Western nations! Recently the mood has turned against the establishment of new industries on the old, large-scale basis and doubts have been amply voiced in the literature cited earlier. That unemployment is hardly ameliorated is of little consequence in countries where purchasing power is sustained by social security payments. On the other hand, there is also less general veneration for those seigneurially placed at the opposite end of the income range. Not that all those in the top financial bracket are, in their vanity, cognizant of the futility of their 'preference drift'. But, starting with Veblen and (for the time being) ending with Hirsch, those living in luxury have been upbraided so much that the enjoyment which, after all, derives from carefree conspicuousness, must have suffered.

However far the distinguished consumer may travel, whether by land, air or sea, to some destination only just included in the brochures, he still runs the risk of meeting his charlady: an increasingly scarce commodity at home, but shunned in foreign parts. 'Positional goods', as Hirsch calls them, lose their attraction when the social position that they represent is occupied by ever larger groups. But this phenomenon also affects the will to strive for such assets. That is the origin of Hirsch's social limits to growth (1977). The disadvantages of living and working in an industrial atmosphere now appear in a different light. The violent opposition to all that can be seen as further investment in a long line of technological innovation, e.g. in a nuclear power plant, originates not so much in a careful consideration of all possible risks as in a general aversion to any further technicalization of industrial society. For many years the conscientious objectors have been listing the now familiar disadvantages: stress on man, strain on nature, poisoning of plants and animals, disturbance of the ecological balance. Indeed, it has all been described years ago in E.M. Forster's classic story: The machine stops. The machine, built by men, has begun to rule their lives. 'We created the machine, to do our will, but we cannot make it do our will now. It has robbed us of the sense of space and the sense of touch; it has blurred every human relation ... paralyzed our bodies and now it compels us to worship it. The machine develops - but not on our lines. *The machine proceeds - but not for our goals'* (1963, 266).

THE ENDS AND THE MEANS

That last sentiment has been of greater concern to the novelist than to the economist: 'our goals'. But this is changing, as a result of the previously described decline in the once-compulsive norms for scientific value freedom. In a recent publication in the series published by the Club of Rome, there is an article by Boulding that harks back to the work of the Dutch futurologist Polak: the development of a community is determined by the visions of the future of a few pioneers, subsequently taken up by a larger circle and now motivating the effort to realize them. 'Certain images capture the social imagination of a people and acquire social resonance' (1977, 298). This theory of social dynamics found little favour at the time, but now, twenty years later, it is hauled from the shelves to counter the growth fetish: 'Those who question mindless growth wish to ... capture the minds of the late twentieth century!' The captivating thought that needs to be propagated is Schumacher's: keep it small! The percentage that reflects the annual growth of the National Product is an insufficient indication of the weal and woe of a society. The United Nations are moving to supplement this quantitative norm with socio-cultural indicators. In a recent thesis on the Antillean economy, Butter suggests that the target of development politics should be determined by human rights as defined in the 1950 Rome Convention (1979). He argues that the text offers a basis for a more narrowly defined goal, that exceeds the purely economic. However, Butter makes the proviso that human dignity be founded on an adequate material basis. After all, as the Dutch say, where there is naught even the emperor loses his rights! Sachs tries a different criterion: according to him the diminishing of social tensions would be a telling indicator of a rising level of prosperity. It has evidently escaped his notice that the conflicts in prosperous nations have in fact increased with the rise in the fortunes of the previously inarticulate working classes (Sachs, 1976).

The problem has been conclusively dealt with by a Polish interdisciplinary group which, in a futuristic tour de force, has attempted to design a long-term model. As the project developed, the need arose to accept an ever-increasing number of hypotheses concerning the influence of previously adhered to values, social structures, and the relevance of exogenous cultural and consumer patterns, with the result that, in the end, the axiological aspects became increasingly obscured (Sachs, 1976). Management decisions to be taken had to be classified according to their adjustability, placed in a fixed timescale and related to each other. The categories that usually suffice: ends and means, input and output, no longer proved appropriate. Finally the crucial question was raised as to the social institutions that would have to undertake management decisions of such moment. Mannheim reached the same point fifty years earlier. 'Who plans the planner?'

Whatever the development plan and whoever the designer, this much is certain - that the choice of technology is the fundamental decision. The problem of the poor nations has rightly been called the challenge of the twentieth century. A social challenge may arouse a variety of responses; Toynbee has described how, throughout the history of cultures, sometimes the correct and sometimes the wrong response has been given.

The answer Western civilization gave to Malthus's problem of the inability of the means to keep up with the demands of an increasing population, derived mainly from technology. The work force required to man the early, labour-intensive, industries was drawn from agriculture. Population growth was low and the industrial demand for labour was high. The apparent parallel observed in backward economies inspired the same answer. However, this time population growth was high and labour demand, because of advances in technology, was low. To this extent the strategy of rapid industrialization was a fallacy.

Meanwhile the answer is still to be found in technology, but it derives from a technology that relates anew to the different conditions now prevailing in the Third World. The challenge of development is met with adjusted, intermediate techniques.

Bibliography

Agosin, M.R. (1976), Economics, welfare and alternative view of man, 'Alternatives', vol. 2, no. 1, pp. 1-22.

Allahwerdi, M.N. (1974), Appropriate technology: what, and for whom?, 'Impact of Science on Society', vol. 24, no. 3, p. 267.

Alvares, C. (1975), 'The interaction of technologies in India. Part 1: Theoretical considerations', TH Eindhoven, 25 November.

Arrêteau, P. (1973), Can the luxury of personal freedom be a reward for work?, 'Impact of Science on Society', vol. 23, no. 4, pp. 307-22.

Arrow, K.J. (1962), The economic implications of learning by doing, 'Review of Economic Studies', vol. 29, no. 80.

Austruy, J. (1968), 'Le Scandale du développement', Paris.

Ayal, E.B. (1963), Value systems and economic development in Japan and Thailand, 'Journal of Social Issues', vol. 19, pp. 35-51.

Banks, A.S. (1974), Industrialization and development: a longitudinal analysis, 'Economic Development and Cultural Change', no. 22, pp. 320-37.

Baranson, J. (1972), 'Multinational Corporations and Developing Country Goals for Technological Self-sufficiency', New York.

Barnett, H.J. (1974), Economic growth and environmental quality are compatible, 'Policy Sciences', no. 5, pp. 137-47.

Barnett, V.M. (1974), Implementation of policies for fuller employment in less developed countries, 'World Development', vol. 2, no. 6, pp. 11-26.

Bass, L.W. (1976), Technical and managerial help for small enterprises, 'World Development', vol. 4, no. 4, pp. 339-47.

Bauer, P.T. (1976), 'Dissent on Development', London.

Bean, A.S., Schiffel, D.D. and Mogee, M.E. (1975), The venture capital market and technological innovation, 'Research Policy', no. 4, pp. 380-408.

Berger, P.L., Berger, B. and Kellner, H. (1974), 'The Homeless Mind', Harmondsworth.

Berliner, J.S. (1962), The feet of the natives are large: An essay on anthropology by an economist, 'Current Anthropology', February, pp. 47-61.

Bernal, J. (1969), 'Science in History', London.

Bhagwat, A. (1973), Main features of the employment problems in developing countries, 'International Monetary Fund Staff Papers', vol. 20, no. 1, pp. 78-99.

Bhalla, A.S. (1974), Technological choice in construction in two Asian Countries: China and India, 'World Development', vol. 2, no. 3, pp. 65-73.

Bhalla, A.S. (ed.) (1975), 'Technology and Employment in Industry', International Labour Office, Geneva.

Bhalla, A.S. (1976), Technology and employment: some conclusions, 'International Labour Review', vol. 113, no. 2, pp. 189-203.

Bhatt, V.V. (1975), On technology policy and its institutional frame, 'World Development', vol. 3, no. 9, pp. 651-63.

Blackaby, F. (1979), 'De-industrialization', London.

Bloom, B. (1964), 'Stability and Change in Human Characteristics', New York.

Bol, D. (1976), Minister Pronk en de doos van Pandora. Commentaar op de nota Bilaterale Ontwikkelingssamenwerking, 'Internationale Spectator', vol. 30, no. 9, pp. 501-13.

Bono, E. de (1967), 'The Use of Lateral Thinking', Harmondsworth.

Boon, G.K. (1964), 'Economic Choice of Human and Physical Factors in Production', The Hague.

Boon, G.K. (1976), Technologische afhankelijkheid. Enige kanttekeningen, 'Internationale Spectator', December, pp. 729-36.

Bos, H.C. (1976), 'An Action Programme for the Selection of Appropriate Industrial Technology. An Introduction', Rotterdam, July.

Boulding, E. (1976), World welfare measurement as social action, 'Alternatives', vol. II, pp. 71-87.

Boulding, E. (1977), Education for inventing the future, in D.L. Meadows (ed.), 'Alternatives to Growth', Cambridge, Mass.

Bowra, M. (1971), 'Periclean Athens', London.

Boyle, G. and R. Harper (eds) (1976), 'Radical Technology', London.

Brameld, T. (1965), Anthropotherapy - Toward theory and

practice, 'Human Organization', vol. 24, no. 1, Spring, pp. 288-97.
Brand, W. (1975), Aangepaste technologie: op- en aanmerkingen. Paper voor de Nuffic conferentie over Wetenschap en Techniek, Leiden, December.
Brand, W. (1977), Alternatieve technieken, 'Bijdrage voor hoofdstuk IV van het ontwerp-advies ter bespreking in de vergadering van 22 februari 1977', Nationale advies raad voor ontwikkelingssamenwerking, The Hague, 14 February.
Brand, W. (1977), 'Ongelijkheid en ontwikkeling', Leiden.
Breit, W. (1973), The development of Clarence Ayres's theoretical institutionalism, 'Social Science Quarterly', pp. 244-57.
Breman, J. (1976), A dualistic labour system? A critique of the 'informal sector' concept, 'Economic and Political Weekly', 27 November, pp. 1870-6.
Breman, J. (1976), A dualistic labour system? A critique of the 'informal sector' concept, 'Economic and Political Weekly', 4 December, pp. 1905-8.
Breman, J. (1976), A dualistic labour system? A critique of the 'informal sector' concept, 'Economic and Political Weekly', 11 December, pp. 1939-44.
Bronckhorst, B. van (1974), Development problems in the perspective of technology. Inaugural address. TH Eindhoven, 22 February.
Bronckhorst, B. van (1976),'Wereldontwikkelingsinspanningen, een schematisch overzicht', Eindhoven.
Brookfield, H. (1975), 'Interdependent Development', London.
Brooks, H. (1973), The state of the art. Technology assessment as a process, 'International Social Science Journal', vol. 25, no. 3, pp. 247-72.
Brouwer, H. and Miedema, J. (1975), 'Zachte techniek. Een onderzoek naar nieuwe vormen van samenleving en economie', Amsterdam.
Brun, O. le (1973), Fundamental aspects of underdevelopment and aims of development, 'University Quarterly', vol. 29, no. 3, pp. 276-91.
Bruton, H.J. (1972), 'The Elasticity of Substitution in Developing Countries', Williams College, Center of Development Economics, Research Memorandum, no. 45, April.
Burnet, F.M. (1972), The implications of global homeostasis, 'Impact of Science on Society', vol. 22, no. 4, pp. 305-15.
Burns, T. (1956), The social character of technology, 'Impact of Science on Society', vol. 7, pp. 147-65.
Burns, T. (1969), Models, images and myths, in W.H.

Gruber and D.G. Marquis (eds), 'Factors in the Transfer of Technology', Cambridge, Mass., pp. 11-23.
Butter, A.J. (1979), 'Wat heet onafhankelijk?', Amsterdam.
Cairncross, A. (1972), Reflections on technological change, 'Scottish Journal of Political Economy', June, pp. 107-14.
Cannegieter, C.A. (1974), Old and new ways of measuring economic progress, 'N.Z. Statistician', December.
Chenery, H. (1974), 'Redistribution with Growth', Oxford.
Clark, N. (1975), The multi-national corporation: The transfer of technology and dependence, 'Development and Change', no. 1, pp. 5-21.
Clarke, R. (1973), The pressing need for alternative technology, 'Impact of Science on Society', vol. 23, no. 4, pp. 257-71.
Congdon, T. (1975), Are we really all Keynesians now?, 'Encounter', April, pp. 23-32.
Cooper, A.C. and Schendel, D. (1976), Strategic responses to technological threats, 'Business Horizons', vol. 19, no. 1, pp. 61-9.
Cooper, C. (1973), Choice of techniques and technological change as problems in political economy, 'International Social Science Journal', vol. 25, no. 3, pp. 293-304.
Cooper, C. (1974), Science policy and technological change in under-developed economies, 'World Development', vol. 2, no. 3, pp. 55-64.
Cooper, C. and Kaplinsky, R. (1974), 'Second-hand Equipment in a Developing Country: A Study of Jute-processing in Kenya', Geneva.
Cooper, Ch. (1972), Science, technology and production in the underdeveloped countries: An introduction, 'Journal of Development Studies', vol. 9, no. 1, pp. 1-18.
Cooper, Ch. (1975), Speech on the occasion of the Nuffic conferentie Wetenschap en techniek voor de ontwikkelingslanden, Leiden, December.
Cross, N., Elliott, D. and Roy, R. (eds) (1974), 'Man-made Future. Readings in Society, Technology and Design', London.
Czepiel, J.A. (1974), Word-of-mouth processes in the diffusion of a major technological innovation, 'Journal of Marketing Research', vol. 11, May, pp. 172-80.
Daly, H.E. (1974), Steady-state economics versus growth mania: A critique of the orthodox conceptions of growth, wants, scarcity, and efficiency, 'Policy Sciences', vol. 5, pp. 149-67.
Dam, A. van (1976), Growth: direction rather than rate, 'Alternatives', vol. 2, pp. 145-50.
Denison, E.F. (1967), 'Why Growth Rates Differ', London.
Dernberger, R.F. (1974), The transfer of technology to China, 'Asia Quarterly', no. 3.

Dickson, D. (1974), 'Alternative Technology and the Politics of Technical Change', London.
Diggins, J.P. (1972), Thoreau, Marx and the 'riddle' of alienation, 'Social Research', vol. 39, pp. 571-98.
Dougherty, C.R.S. (1974), On the secular macro-economic consequences of technical progress, 'Economic Journal', vol, 84, no. 335, pp. 543-65.
Drissel, J.P. (1972), Why the world will shift to intermediate technology. An interview with George McRobie, 'Futurist', vol. 11, no. 2, pp. 83-6.
Drobyshev, M. and Vafa, A. (1974), Technological progress and spiritual culture in the countries of the 'third world', 'Asian Survey', vol. 14, no. 3, pp. 207-19.
Drucker, P. (1973), 'Landmarks of To-morrow', New York.
Duller, H.J.M. (1970), 'Ekonomische ontwikkeling en ondernemerschap', The Hague.
Duller, H.J.M. (1973), De economie van Suriname, 'Intermediair', 9 and 16 March.
Duller, H.J.M. (1975), 'Antilliaanse economie en ondernemerschap', Instituut voor culturele antropologie en sociologie der niet-westerse volken, publikatie no. 13, Leiden.
Duller, H.J.M. (1976), 'The climate of environment', Instituut voor culturele antropologie en sociologie der niet-westerse volken, publikatie no. 15, Leiden.
Duller, H.J.M. (1977), 'Zachte techniek - een hard gelag?', Instituut voor culturele antropologie en sociologie der niet-westerse volken, publikatie no. 25, Leiden.
Durbin, P.T. (1972), Technology and values: A philosopher's perspective, 'Technology and Culture', vol. 13, no. 4, pp. 556-76.
Duvignaud, J. (1970), 'Change at Shebika', London.
Eckstein, A. (1966), 'Communist China's Economic Growth and Foreign Trade', New York.
'Economist, The' (1975), Russian farming. Why do they need imports at all?, 'The Economist', 18 October.
'Economist, The' (1976a), Why Russians will have to keep walking, 'The Economist', 31 January.
'Economist, The' (1976b), Brezhnev's Russia. The great breakthrough that never breaks, 'The Economist', 14 February.
'Economist, The' (1977), Where have all the beavers gone?, 'The Economist', 31 December.
'Economist, The' (1978a), The continental challenge, 'The Economist', 4 February.
'Economist, The' (1978b), The pain of old ideas, 'The Economist', 4 March.
'Economist, The' (1978c), Back to back. A survey of Kenya and Tanzania, 'The Economist', 11 March.

'Economist, The' (1978d), Revolution it isn't but it can be green for everyone, 'The Economist', 13 May.
Edel, M. (1970), Innovative supply: A weak point in economic development theory, 'Social Sciences Information', vol. 9, no, 3, pp. 9-40.
Eindhoven (1975), Aanbevelingen en opmerkingen van de subthemagroepen van de delegatie van de Technische Hogeschool Eindhoven naar de Nationale Nuffic Conferentie, 15-17 December 1975 in Leiden, Eindhoven, 14 November.
Ekstein, A. (1966), 'Communist China's Growth and Foreign Trade', New York.
Ellul, J. (1964), 'The Technological Society', New York.
Entrepreneurial research planning workshop (1975), 'Entrepreneurial development in low-income communities: Research plan and working proposals', East-west technology and development institute, Honolulu, July.
Feibleman, J.K. (1967), The philosophy of tools, 'Social Forces', vol. 45, no. 3, pp. 329-37.
Feld, B.T. (1974), Draft code of conduct on transfer of technology, 'World Development', vol. 2, nos 4 and 5, pp. 77-82.
Ferkiss, V. (1973), 'Technological Man', New York.
Fiegehen, G.C., Lansley, P.S. and Smith, A.D. (1977), 'Poverty and Progress in Britain 1953-1973', Cambridge.
Fleming, D. (1972), Roots of the new conservation movement, 'Perspectives in American History', vol. 6, pp. 7-91.
Forbes, R.J. (1968), 'The Conquest of Nature: Technology and its consequences', London.
Forrester, J. (1972), 'World Dynamics', American Academy of Arts and Sciences Bulletin, no. 25, April.
Forster, E.M., The machine stops, in A.O. Lewis (ed.), 'Of men and machines', New York, 1963.
Forsyth, D.J.C., McBain, N.S. and Pickett, J. (1974), The choice of technology, economic efficiency and employment in developing countries, 'World Development', vol. 2, no. 3, pp. 47-54.
Foster, G.A. (1965), Peasant society and the image of limited good, 'American Anthropologist', vol. 67.
Frank, A.G. (1976), 'Capitalism and Underdevelopment in Latin-America: Historical Studies of Chile and Brazil', New York.
Freeman, C. (1974), 'The Economics of Industrial Innovation', Harmondsworth.
Freeman, C., Oldham, C.H.G., Cooper, C.M., Sinclair, T.C. and Achilladelis, B.G. (1971), The goals of R & D in the 1970's. Discussion paper, 'Science Studies', no. 1, pp. 357-406.

Frick, R.K. (1976), Development planning: The systematic application of technological innovation, 'Operational Research Quarterly', vol. 27, no. 1, pp. 199-207.
Galenson, W. and Leibenstein, H. (1955), Investment criteria, productivity and economic development, 'Quarterly Journal of Economics', August.
Galbraith, J.K. (1971), 'Economics, Peace and Laughter. A Contemporary Guide', Harmondsworth.
Galtung, J., Guha, A., Wirak, A., Sjlie, S., Cifuentes, M. and Goldstein, H. (1975), Measuring world development - II, 'Alternatives', vol. 1, pp. 523-55.
Gartner, J. and Naiman, Ch.S. (1976), Overcoming the barriers to technology transfer, 'Research Management', March, pp. 22-8.
Geertz, C. (1963), 'Peddlers and Princes;Social Change and Economic Modernization in Two Indonesian Towns', Chicago.
Gouldner, A.W. (1974), The metaphoricality of marxism and the context-freeing grammar of socialism, 'Theory and Society', vol. 1, no. 4, pp. 387-414.
Gruber, W.H. and Marquis, D.G. (eds) (1969), 'Factors in the Transfer of Technology', Cambridge.
Gruber, W.H. (1969), The development and utilization of technology in industry, in W.H. Gruber and D.G. Marquis (eds), 'Factors in the Transfer of Technology', Cambridge, pp. 39-95.
Grunberg, E. (1964), The profit maximization assumption. Comment, 'Oxford Economic Papers', no. 2, July, pp. 286-90.
Gustafson, W.E. (1962), Research and development, new products and productivity change, 'American Economic Review Proceedings', vol. 52, p. 177.
Habbakkuk, H.J. (1976), 'American and British Technology in the Nineteenth Century. The Search for Labour-saving Inventions', Cambridge.
Hallis, M. (1975), 'Rational Economic Man', Cambridge.
Handwerker, W.P. (1973), Technology and household configuration in urban Africa: The Bassa of Monrovia, 'American Sociological Review', vol. 38, no. 2, pp. 182-97.
Harper, P. (1973), In search of allies for the soft technologies, 'Impact of Science on Society', vol. 23, no. 4, pp. 287-305.
Haq, M. ul (1971), Employment in the 1970's: A new perspective, 'International Development Review', vol. 13, pp. 9-13.
Harris, J.R. and Todaro, M.P. (1970), Migration, unemployment and development, 'American Economic Review', vol. 60, March.
De Hastings, C. (1980), 'The Alternative Society', London.

Healey, D.T. (1972), Development policy: New thinking about an interpretation, 'Journal of Economic Literature', vol. 10, no. 3, pp. 757-97.
Heertje, A. (1973), 'Economie en technische ontwikkeling', Leiden.
Heierli, U. (1976), Toward a low-energy development concept for the third world, 'Alternatives', vol. 2, pp. 39-60.
Helleiner, G.K. (1975), The role of multinational corporations in the less developed countries' trade in technology, 'World Development', vol. 3, pp. 161-89.
Herel, G. van (1976), 'Overdracht van technologie naar ontwikkelingslanden en het beleid van de Andesgroep', Werkdocument van het Instituut voor Ontwikkelingsvraagstukken, no. 13, Tilburg.
Higgins, B. (1959), 'Economic Development', London.
Hill, P. (1977), 'Population, Prosperity and Poverty', London.
Hill, C.T. and Utterback, J.M. (1979), 'Technological Innovation for a Dynamic Economy', Oxford.
Hirsch, F. (1977), 'Social Limits to Growth', London.
Hoda, M. (1973), Development is a two-way street to survival, 'Impact of Science on Society', vol. 23, no. 4, pp. 273-85.
Homans, G.C. (1964), Bringing men back in, 'American Sociological Review', vol. 29, no. 5, pp. 805-18.
Hoogvelt, A.M.M. and Child, D. (1973), Rhodesia: Economic blockade and development, 'Monthly Review', vol. 25, no. 5, pp. 41-50.
Hoselitz, B.F. (1962), 'Sociological Aspects of Economic Growth', Chicago.
Illich, I. (1973), 'Tools for Conviviality', London.
Inkeles, A. and Smith, D.H. (1974), 'Becoming Modern. Individual Change in Six Developing Countries', London.
International Labour Office (1971), 'Labour Force Projections 1965-1985', Geneva.
International Labour Office (1972), 'Employment, Incomes and Equality, A Strategy for Increasing Productive Employment in Kenya', Geneva.
International Labour Office (1973), 'The Role of the Textile Industry in the Expansion of Employment in Developing Countries', Geneva.
Jacob, E. (1976), Causes of under-utilization of production capacities in industry and their effects on the reproduction process of selected developing countries, 'Wissenschaftliche Beiträge', vol. 11, no. 1, pp. 5-21.
James, J. (1976), A report on a pilot investigation of the choice of technology in developing countries, 'World Development', vol. 4, no. 5, pp. 457-8.

Jenks, W. (1972), 'Technology for Freedom. Man in his Environment. The ILO Contribution', International Labour Office, Geneva.
Jéquier, N. (1976), 'Appropriate Technology. Problems and Promises', OECD publication, Paris.
Johnson, H.G. (1975), 'Technology and Economic Interdependence', London.
Johnston, F. (1967), Agriculture and structural transformation in developing countries: A survey of research, 'Journal of Economic Literature', pp. 369-98.
Jones, A.T. (1976), Output, employment and labour productivity in Europe since 1955, 'National Institute Economic Review', August.
Jones, G. (1971), 'The Role of Science and Technology in Developing Countries', London.
Kahn, H., Brown, W. and Martel, L. (1976), 'The Next 2000 years: A Scenario for America and the World', New York.
Kaldor, N. (1965), The role of taxation in economic development, in E.A.G. Robinson (ed.), 'Problems in Economic Development', London, p. 170.
Kennedy, P. (1976), Cultural factors affecting entrepreneurship and development in the informal economy in Ghana, 'IDS Bulletin (ISS)', vol. 8, no. 2, pp. 17-21.
Keynes, J.M. (1936), 'General Theory of Employment, Interest and Money', London.
Kindleberger, C.P. (1965), 'Economic Development', New York.
Kindleberger, C.P. (1973), The great transformation by Karl Polanyi, 'Daedalus', vol. 103, no. 1, pp. 45-52.
Kingston, W. (1977), 'Innovation', London.
Koentjaraningrat (1975), 'Anthropology in Indonesia, A Bibliographical Review', The Hague.
Koplin, H. (1963), The profit maximization assumption, 'Oxford Economic Papers', vol. 15, pp. 130-9.
Korthals Altes, F.W. (1975), 'Seminar: Een begin van aangepaste technologie in de Technische Hogeschool Eindhoven, 22-23 April 1975', Koninklijk instituut voor de tropen, afdeling agrarisch onderzoek, Amsterdam.
Kriesberg, L. (1963), Entrepreneurs in Latin America and the role of cultural and situational processes, 'International Social Science Journal', vol. 15.
Kuznets, S. (1965), Postwar economic growth: four lectures '65, 'Economicae', vol. 32, no. 128.
Labovitz, S. (1975), Some implications of technological change and territorial differentiation for underdeveloped countries, 'Journal of Comparative Family Studies', vol. 6, no. 1, pp. 101-10.
Lall, S. (1975), Is 'dependence' a useful concept in analysing under-development?, 'World Development', vol. 3, nos 11 and 12, pp. 799-810.

Lall, S. and Streeten, P. (1977), 'Foreign Investment, Transnationals and Developing Countries', London.

Layton, E.T. (1974), Technology as knowledge, 'Technology & Culture', vol. 15, pp. 31-41.

Leibenstein, H. (1978), 'General X-efficiency Theory and Economic Development', Oxford.

Leis, P.E. (1964), Yaw enculturation: A reexamination of the early learning hypothesis, 'Southwestern Journal of Anthropology', vol. 20, pp. 32-41.

Lerner, D. (1974), 'The Passing of Traditional Society', New York.

Lewis, J. (1972), Overview, in 'Technology and Economics in International Development; Report of a seminar', Office of Science and Technology, USAID.

Lewis, R.A. (1972), Some aspects of the research and development effort of the Soviet Union, 1924-35, 'Science Studies', vol. 2, pp. 153-79.

Lewis, W.A. (1957), 'The Theory of Economic Growth', London.

Lianos, T.P. (1975), Capital-labor substitution in a developing country. The case of Greece', European Economic Review', vol. 6, pp. 129-41.

Linneman, H. (1975), Food for a doubling world population. 'A study of the long-term food-situation', Working-paper t.b.v. de NAR studiedag op 11 November, The Hague.

Lipton, M. (1977), 'Why Poor People Stay Poor. A Study of Urban Bias in World Development', London.

Lloyd, P. (1974), Class consciousness in the third world, 'New Society', vol. 30.

Love, S. (1977), The new look of the future, 'Futurist', vol. 11, no. 2, pp. 78-80.

Luders, R. and Cabero, N. (1970), 'Employment and Technology in Industry. The Chilean Case', ILO, Geneva.

Lund letter (1977), 'The Lund Letter and Report on Science, Technology and Basic Human Needs', Nationale adviesraad voor ontwikkelingssamenwerking, 13 September.

McCall, S. (1975), Quality of life, 'Social Indicators Research', vol. 2, pp. 229-48.

McClelland, D.C. (1969), The role of achievement orientation in the transfer of technology, in W.H. Gruber and D.G. Marquis (eds), 'Factors in the Transfer of Technology', Cambridge, pp. 61-88.

McClelland, D.C. and Winter, D. (1969), 'Motivating Economic Achievement', Geneva.

Macrae, N. (1975), America's third century, 'The Economist', 25 October.

Machlup, F. (1962), 'The Production and Distribution of Knowledge in the United States', Princeton.

Madge, Ch. (1978), Drawing the poverty line, 'Times Literary Supplement', 27 January.
Mansfield, E. (1975), International technology transfer: Forms, resource requirements, and policies, 'American Economic Review', May, pp. 372-6.
Mansilla, H.C.F. (1974), Kritik der Modernisierungs- und Dependenztheorien, 'Soziale Welt', vol. 25, no. 2, pp. 209, 223.
Marceau, J. (1977), 'Class and Status in France. Economic Change and Social Immobility 1945-1975', Oxford.
Marien, M. (1977), The two visions of post-industrial society, 'Futures', October, pp. 415-31.
Maselli, G. (1977), 'Transfer of Technology through International Movements of Manpower', REMP Bulletin, September.
Maslow, A.H. (1962), 'Towards a Psychology of Being', Princeton.
Mason, R. Hal. (1971), 'The Transfer of Technology and the Factor Proportions Problem: The Philippines and Mexico', UNITAR research reports no. 10, New York.
Mathias, P. (1972), Who unbound Prometheus? Science and technical change, 1600-1800, in A.E. Musson (ed.), 'Science, Technology and Economic Growth in the Nineteenth Century', London.
Mazrui, A.A. (1975), Eclecticism as an ideological alternative: An African perspective, 'Alternatives', vol. 1, pp. 465-86.
Meier, G.M. (1971), Rationale of capital allocation - Note, in G.M. Meier (ed.), 'Leading Issues in Economic Development', 2nd edn, pp. 333-9.
Mead, M. (1956), 'New Lives for Old; Cultural Transformation: Manus 1928-'53', London.
Mead, M. (1970-2), Some cultural anthropological responses to technical assistance experience, 'Social Science Information', vol. 9, no. 6, pp. 49-59.
Meadows, D.H., Meadows, D.L., Randers, J. and Behrens, W.W. (1972), 'The Limits to Growth', New York.
Meadows, P. (1973), Development: Some perspective orientations, 'International Journal of Comparative Sociology', vol. 14, nos 1 and 2, pp. 19-34.
Merens-Riedstra, H.S. and Stroink, P.L. (1972), Werkloosheid of arbeid als sociaal probleem, 'Mens en onderneming', vol. 26, no. 5, pp. 279-83.
Merill, R.S. (1972), The role of technology in cultural evolution, 'Social Biology', vol. 19, no. 3, pp. 240-7.
Millan, P. and Schydlowsky, D.M. (1973), 'Macro-economic Consequences of Multiple Shifting: An Input-Output Approach', Boston.
Mishan, E.J. (1960), Review article, 'Economica', May.

Mishan, E.J. (1977), 'The Economic Growth Debate. An Assessment', London.
Morawetz, D. (1974), Employment implications of industrialization in developing countries: A survey, 'Economic Journal', September.
Morley, S.A. and Smith, G.W. (1974), 'Managerial Discretion and the Choice of Technology by Multinational Firms in Brazil', Rice University, Houston.
Morley, S.A. and Smith, G.W. (1977), The choice of technology: multinational firms in Brazil, 'Economic Development and Cultural Change', pp. 239-64.
Mulkay, M.J. (1972), 'The Social Process of Innovation', London.
Musson, A.E. (1972), The diffusion of technology in Great Britain during the industrial revolution, in A.E. Musson (ed.), 'Science, Technology and Economic Growth', London.
Myrdal, G. (1968), 'Asian Drama: An Inquiry into the Poverty of Nations', London.
Naipaul, V.S. (1977), 'India: A Wounded Civilization', London.
Netherlands Economic Institute (1957), 'Alternative Techniques of Production', Rotterdam.
Nash, M. (1961), The social context of economic choice in a small society, 'Man', no. 219, pp. 186-90.
Nationale Advies Raad voor Ontwikkelingssamenwerking (1977), 'Ontwerpadvies overdracht van wetenschap en techniek naar ontwikkelingslanden', The Hague, 12 December.
Neersø, P. (1975), Some aspects of India's policies on the import of technology, 'Development and Change', no. 1, pp. 41-55.
Neumann, M. (1976), Innovationen, Wachstum und Freizeit, 'Kyklos', vol. 29, pp. 639-59.
Niehoff, A.H. and Anderson, J.C. (1964), The process of cross-cultural innovation, 'International Development Review', vol. 6, pp. 5-11.
Nieuwenhuijze, C.A.O. van (1976), Verschuivingen in het denken over ontwikkelingsbeleid, 'Internationale spectator', vol. 30, no. 9, pp. 524-8.
Nisbet, R. (1972a), Radicalism as therapy, 'Encounter', March, pp. 53-80.
Nisbet, R. (1972b), The nemesis of authority, 'Encounter', August, pp. 11-21.
Nuffic (1975), 'Rapport van de werkgroep onderzoeksbijstand', The Hague, 8 August.
Nurkse, R. (1953), 'Problems of Capital Formation in Underdeveloped Countries', London.
Oldak, P. (1972), Scientific-technical progress and the

limits to economic analysis, 'Problems of Economics', April, pp. 3-23.
Omo-Fadaka, J. (1975), Development: The third way, 'Alternatives', vol. 1, pp. 23-53.
Oort, P.D.E.M. van (1978), Aangepaste technologie. Een kritische analyse, 'Doctoraal'-thesis Sociology of Non-western Societies, Leiden.
Orr, D.W. (1976), Scarcity and the future of politics, 'Alternatives', vol. 2, pp. 135-44.
Pacey, A. (1975), 'The Maze of Ingenuity', New York.
Pak, N.K. (1975), The impact of technology on the youth of developing countries, 'Impact of Science on Society', vol. 25, no. 4, pp. 307-11.
Parthasarathi, A. (1979), Technological bridgeheads for self-reliant development, 'Development Dialogue', vol. 1.
Pen, J. (1974), 'Income Distribution', Harmondsworth.
Pen, J. (1977), in J. Tinbergen (ed.), 'Naar een rechtvaardiger inkomensverdeling', Amsterdam.
Peters, E.B. (1975), Cultural and language obstacles to information transfer in the scientific and technical field, 'Management International Review', vol. 15, no. 1, pp. 75-88.
Pettman, J. (1975), Development through self-reliance, 'Australian and New Zealand Journal of Sociology', vol. 11, no. 1, pp. 42-3.
Phelps-Brown, E.H. (1973), Levels and movements of industrial productivity and real wages internationally compared 1860-1970, 'Economic Journal', vol. 83, March.
Pickett, J., Forsyth, D.J.C. and McBain, N.S. (1974), The choice of technology, economic efficiency and employment in developing countries, 'World Development', vol. 2, no. 3, pp. 47-54.
Playfair, L. (1852), 'Lectures on the Results of the Great Exhibition of 1852', London.
Pohlman, J.E. (1972), Another look at capital- and labor-intensive technology in developing countries, 'Journal of Economic Issues', vol. 6, pp. 158-65.
Quarles van Ufford, P. (1976), De culturele context van ontwikkeling. Enkele sociaal-wetenschappelijke opvattingen over de relatie tussen cultuur en ontwikkeling op Java, 'Internationale spectator', vol. 30, no. 12, pp. 721-8.
Ramaer, J.C. (1976), A discussion paper on: The choice of appropriate technology, development and capital saving, 'Nationale advies raad voor ontwikkelingssamenwerking', 15 October.
Ranger, T. (1977), The invention of tradition in colonial Africa, 'Past and Present Conference 1977 on The Invention of Tradition', Oxford, 4 July, pp. 55-86.

Rattner, H. (1975), Développement et emploi: la viabilité d'une technologie intermédiaire, 'Revue tiers monde', vol. 16, no. 62, pp. 295-310.

Rees-Mogg, W. (1977), 'William Rees-Mogg Analyses the Equation of British Poverty. One Dutch Man Hour = Two British Man Hours', Times Newspapers, 23 September.

Rhyne, R. (1974), Technological forecasting within alternative whole futures projections, 'Technological Forecasting and Social Change', vol. 6, pp. 133-62.

Riesman, D. (1952), 'The Lonely Crowd', New Haven.

Rifkin, S.B. (1975), The Chinese model for science and technology: Its relevance for other developing countries, 'Technological Forecasting and Social Change', vol. 7, no. 3, pp. 257-71.

Roberts, E.B. (1969), Entrepreneurship and technology, in W.H. Gruber and W.G. Marquis (eds), 'Some Factors in the Transfer of Technology', Cambridge, pp. 219-37.

Roman, D. (1974), Technology, the key to market expansion for developing countries, 'Industrial Marketing Management', vol. 3, pp. 167-76.

Rosenberg, N. (1976), 'Perspectives on Technology', Cambridge.

Rullière, G. (1971), Le rôle des phénomènes d'ostentation dans les pays économiquement développés, 'Cahier de sociologie économique', vol. 2, no. 2, pp. 123-214.

Rürup, R. (1974), Historians and modern technology. Reflections on the development and current problems of the history of technology, 'Technology and Culture', vol. 15, pp. 161-93.

Sachs, I. (1973), Development, environment and technology assessment, 'International Social Science Journal', vol. 25, no. 3, pp. 273-83.

Sachs, I. (1976), 'The discovery of the third world', Cambridge, Mass.

Sagasti, F.R. (1973), Underdevelopment, science and technology: The point of view of the underdeveloped countries, 'Science Studies', vol. 3, pp. 47-59.

Sagasti, F.R. (1975), The ITINTEC system for industrial technology policy in Peru, 'World Development', vol. 3, nos 11 and 12, pp. 867-76.

Sagasti, F.R. (1979), Towards endogenous science and technology for another development, 'Development Dialogue', vol. 1.

Sahlin, M. (1972), 'Stone Age Economics', London.

Saito, M. (1974), Technology transfer as a development strategy in the region, 'Economic Bulletin for Asia and the Far East', no. 1, pp. 33-41.

Samuelson, P.A. (1976), 'Economics', New York.

Schiavo-Campo, S. and Singer, H.W. (1970), 'Perspectives of Economic Development', Boston.

Schumacher, E.F. (1974), 'Small is Beautiful', London.
Schumacher, E.F. (1975), Alternatives in technology, 'Alternatives', vol. 1, no. 1, pp. 7-22.
Schumacher, E.F. (no date), 'Social and Economic Problems Calling for the Development of Intermediate Technology', London.
Schumacher, E.F. (1977), 'A Guide for the Perplexed', London.
Schumpeter, J.A. (1944), 'Capitalism, Socialism and Democracy', London.
Scitovsky, T. (1976), 'The Joyless Economy. An Inquiry into Human Satisfaction and Consumer Dissatisfaction', Oxford.
Selwyn, P. (1973), The tyranny of the technician, 'International Development Review', vol. 15, no. 1, pp. 17-20.
Sen, A. (1975), Employment, institutions and technology: Some policy issues, 'International Labour Review', vol. 112, no. 1, pp. 45-73.
Sen, A. (1975), 'Employment, Technology and Development. A Study Prepared for the ILO Within the Framework of the World Employment Programme', Oxford.
Servan-Schreiber, J.J. (1967), 'Le défit Américain', Paris.
Shonfield, A. (1960), 'The Attack on World Poverty', London.
Shriver, D.W. (1972), Man and his machines: Four angles of vision, 'Technology and Culture', vol. 13, no. 4, pp. 531-55.
Sigurdson, J. (1973), The suitability of technology in contemporary China, 'Impact of Science on Society', vol. 23, no. 4, pp. 341-52.
Sigurdson, J. (1974), Technology and employment in China, 'World Development', vol. 2, no. 3, pp. 75-85.
Sinclair, S.W. (1976), The 'intermediate' sector in the economy, 'Manpower and Unemployment Research', vol. 9, no. 2, pp. 55-63.
Singer, H.W. (1972), The technology gap and the developing countries, 'International Journal of Environmental Studies', vol. 3, pp. 119-23.
Singer, H.W. (1977a), Appropriate technology for a basic human needs strategy, 'International Development Review', vol. 19, no. 2, pp. 8-11.
Singer, H.W. (1977b), 'Technologies For Basic Needs', ILO publication, Geneva.
Slotkin, J. (1960), 'From Field to Factory', Chicago.
Stewart, F. (1972), Choice of technique in developing countries, 'Journal of Development Studies', vol. 9, pp. 99-121.

Stewart, F. (1974), Technology and employment in LDC's, 'World Development', vol. 2, no. 3, pp. 17-46.
Stewart, F. (1977), 'Technology and Underdevelopment', London.
Stewart, F. and Streeten, (1971), Conflicts between output and employment objectives in developing countries, 'Oxford Economic Papers', vol. 23, no. 2, pp. 145-68.
Stokes, E. (1978), Images of India, 'Times Literary Supplement', 3 February.
Strassman, W.P. (1968), 'Technological Change and Economic Development', New York.
Streeten, P. (1972), Technology gaps between rich and poor countries, 'Scottish Journal of Political Economy', November, pp. 213-30.
Streeten, P. (1974), The limits of development research, 'World Development', vol. 2, nos 10-12, pp. 1-24.
Streeten, P. (1975), Industrialization in a unified development strategy, 'World Development', vol. 3, no. 1, pp. 1-9.
Streeten, P. and Lall, S. (1973), 'The Flow of Financial Resources: Private Foreign Investment. Main findings of a Study of Private Foreign Investment in Selected Developing Countries', UNCTAD.
Sussex Manifesto (1974), 'Science and Technology to Developing Countries during the Second Development Decade', Brighton.
Taviss, I. (1972), A survey of popular attitudes toward technology, 'Technology and Culture', vol. 13, no. 4, pp. 606-21.
'Technology for Freedom' (1972), ILO, Geneva.
Templin, R.T. (1972), New, yet old, sociology of critical theory: The 'economic means', 'Journal of Human Relations', vol. 20, nos 1 and 2, pp. 124-40.
TH Twente (1975), 'Aangepaste technieken. Nota van een voorbereidingsgroep van de TH Twente', Nuffic-conferentie, Leiden, December.
Thomas, T. (1977), 'Relevant Technology. Speech at the Annual Meeting of Hindustan Lever Limited, held at Bombay on Thursday 24 June 1976', Nationale advies raad voor ontwikkelingssamenwerking, 23 February.
Timmer, C.P., Thomas, J.W., Wells, L.T. and Morawetz, D. (1975), 'The Choice of Technology in Developing Countries', Boston.
Tinbergen, J. (1973), 'The Human Dimensions of Economic Growth', New Delhi.
Tinbergen, J. (1975), 'The Need for a Quantitative Framework: 1970 as a Starting Point'. Working paper t.b.v. de NAR-studiedag op 11 November 1975. Nationale advies raad voor ontwikkelingssamenwerking, 20 October.

TOOL (1976), 'Congress Socially Appropriate Technology', Speeches and papers delivered during the congress organized by the TOOL Foundation at the Catholic University of Nijmegen, 13-14 February, Amsterdam.

Toulmin, S. (1969), Innovation and utilization, in W.H. Gruber and D.G. Marquis (eds), 'Factors in the Transfer of Technology', Cambridge, p. 37.

Uchendu, V.C. (1975), The role of intermediate technology in East African agricultural development, 'East African Journal of Rural Development', vol. 8, nos 1 and 2, pp. 181-90.

US Government (1976), 'The Measure of Poverty', Washington.

Utterback, J.M. (1975), The role of applied research institutes in the transfer of technology in Latin America, 'World Development', vol. 3, no. 9, pp. 665-73.

Volkov, M. (1975), The developing countries: The choice of technology, 'Problems of Economics', no. 4, pp. 3-25.

Wakefield, R.A. and Stafford, P. (1977), Appropriate technology. What it is and where it is going, 'Futurist', vol. 11, no. 2, pp. 72-6.

Watson, R.A. (1975), The limits of world order, 'Alternatives', vol. 1, pp. 487-513.

Weeks, J. (1971), Wage policy and the colonial legacy - a comparative study, 'Journal of Modern African Studies', vol. 9.

Wegener, H. (1976), Technologietransfer von Industriestaaten in Entwicklungsländer, 'Europa-Archiv', vol. 31, no. 16, pp. 527-39.

Weisskoff, R., Levy, R., Nisonoff, L. and Wolff, E. (1973), 'A Multi-sector Simulation Model of Employment, Growth and Income Distribution in Puerto Rico: A Re-evaluation of a "Successful" Development Strategy', Cambridge, Mass.

Wells, L.T. (1974), Don't overautomate your foreign plant, 'Harvard Business Review', January-February, pp. 111-18.

Wetenschappelijke raad voor het regeringsbeleid (1977), 'Maken wij er werk van', The Hague, publikatie no. 13.

White, L.J. (1976), Appropriate technology, X-inefficiency, and a competitive environment: Some evidence from Pakistan, 'Quarterly Journal of Economics', vol. 90, no. 4, pp. 575-89.

Whitehead, A.N. (1925), 'Science and the Modern World', New York.

Wilde, T. de (1975), 'Inleiding Aangepaste Technologie t.b.v. Nuffic/RUL Conferentie 1975', Eindhoven, September.

Williams, B.R. (ed.) (1973), 'Science and Technology in Economic Growth', London.
Winston, G.C. (1971), Capital utilization in economic development, 'Economic Journal', March, vol. 81.
Wionczek, M.S. (1976), Technology transfer. What do the developing countries want?, 'Intereconomics', no. 3, pp. 76-9.
Zimmerman, L.J. (1975), Non-monetary capital formation and rural development, 'World Development', vol. 3, no. 6, pp. 414-19.
Zuthem, H.J. van (1969), 'De Geloofwaardigheid van onze economische orde', Delft.

Index

Basic needs, 31, 63, 64, 66ff, 77, 86, 160

Capital (capital-coefficient), 22, 83, 84, 111, 165
Capitalization (mechanization), 17, 21, 28, 31, 82, 84, 85, 97, 124
Centre-periphery, 27, 37, 52, 159; see also Dependence
Chinese model, 99, 101, 117, 144, 152
Compensation, theory of, 21, 22, 97ff
Cost analysis, 29, 30, 35, 43

Dependence, 35, 40, 87ff, 123, 126, 129, 144; see also Centre-periphery
Dualism, 107, 127, 145, 146

Ecology, 15, 16, 22, 41
Economic growth (development), 5, 10, 23, 55, 56, 70, 71, 99, 101, 153, 161
Employment (unemployment), 21, 22, 29, 76, 84, 92ff, 96ff, 143, 169

Entrepreneurship, 86, 138ff
Export strategy, 34ff

Green revolution, 74, 104, 105, 147, 165

Import substitution, 36ff, 49, 52, 76
Income distribution, 10, 29, 38, 40, 62, 68ff, 104, 143; see also Trickling-down effect
Infant industry, 36, 40, 81, 124, 146
Informal sector, 85, 86, 140
Invention (innovation, technical progress), 5, 21ff, 27, 82, 128, 129, 138, 157ff, 167, 170
Investment, 81ff, 137, 168

Labour (labour productivity), 17, 18, 21, 30, 40, 42, 44, 49, 106, 108, 110, 124, 126ff, 145
Learning process, 44, 80, 124, 149, 158, 165ff
'Limited good', 48, 133, 134

Modernization, 11, 28, 31,

106, 114ff, 122, 125, 136, 143
Multinationals, 40, 42ff, 53, 86, 90, 145, 146

Patents (licence-charter), 33, 34, 39, 40, 49
Product cycle, 23, 26, 27, 35, 159
Post-industrial society, 2, 3, 7, 134, 144

Quality control, 28, 31, 35, 86, 101

Rationality, 20, 33, 47, 48, 112ff, 131
Research and Development, 11, 28, 39, 128, 129, 146, 151ff
Royalties, 39, 40, 49, 146

Second-hand equipment, 79ff
Shadow prices, 50, 51, 111
Social legislation, 49, 50, 85

Trade unions, 49, 50, 71, 103, 145
Trickling-down effect, 71, 75, 104; see also Income distribution
Turnkey plants, 23, 31

Underutilization (excess capacity), 46ff

Zero growth, 4, 5, 15, 52, 55, 131, 134, 141

For Product Safety Concerns and Information please contact our EU representative GPSR@taylorandfrancis.com
Taylor & Francis Verlag GmbH, Kaufingerstraße 24, 80331 München, Germany

www.ingramcontent.com/pod-product-compliance
Lightning Source LLC
LaVergne TN
LVHW010619300926
849162LV00001B/3
9781041268116